Steam Memories: 1950's – 1960's

No. 106: LEEDS AND DISTRICT EN

David Dunn

INTRODUCTION

This first part of a two-part album covering the Leeds area engine sheds could also be entitled West Riding engine sheds but Leeds won the day. We have included sheds from the BR shed groups 55 and 56, not in any order but both number groups are represented totally.

In this tome we have Holbeck, Stourton, Ardsley, Copley Hill, Farnley Junction and Normanton. Pt.2 will include Bradford, Low Moor, Sowerby Bridge, Mirfield, Wakefield, Royston, Manningham, and Huddersfield. An eclectic mixture featuring former Great Northern, Lancashire & Yorkshire, London Midland & Scottish, Midland Railway, and London & North Western engine sheds.

Readers might be wondering where Neville Hill shed has got to. Well that former North Eastern Railway establishment was covered in the album – No.92 in this series – featuring the York area 50 Group engine sheds as 50B.

Enjoy the variety of locomotives, buildings, and facilities once found in these dirty, filthy, sulphurous, smoky, magical temples of industrial gems when steam attracted enthusiasts in their hundreds of thousands every weekend and some – especially the photographers – during the week too!

David Dunn, Cramlington, June 2019

(*cover*) 1Fs Nos.41661 and 41844 along with a couple of 3F 0-6-0Ts - all residents - spend the weekend at Normanton shed on Sunday 21st August 1955. *F.W. Hampson (ARPT)*.

(*previous page*) Kentish Town based 'Royal Scot' No.46133 THE GREEN HOWARDS gracing the yard at Holbeck during a visit on a murky Sunday 13th November 1960. The 7P had by now clocked-up nearly two-and-a-half million revenue earning miles and was due a visit to works to get that cylinder cover looked at! *Raymond Embleton*.

Printed and bound by The Amadeus Press, Cleckheaton, West Yorkshire
First published in the United Kingdom by Book Law Publications, 382 Carlton Hill, Nottingham, NG4 1JA

All different! Resident Ivatt Cl.4 No.43043, Kingmoor 'Royal Scot' No.46162 QUEEN'S WESTMINSTER RIFLEMAN, Stanier Cl.5 No.44854 another resident, Carnforth 'Jubilee' No.45587 BARODA, and Rowsley BR Std. 9F No.92048 constitute a cosy get-together around the turntable in No.2 roundhouse in 1963. Note that all except the 2-10-0 have ATC/AWS fitted. *Malcolm Foreman*.

It was late in the day for this Fowler Cl.4 tank. It is 7th November 1965 – hence the lights, even in broad daylight – and the numbers of the 2-6-4T still active were falling weekly. At the height of the previous summer less than a dozen were still working. No.42394 eventually became the penultimate operational member of the class and was withdrawn in June 1966. The distinction of being the last of class – it's queer how none of these useful locomotives were preserved yet we have Panniers coming out of the woodwork everywhere! – went to Huddersfield's No.42410 which was finally dispatched during the following September. *A.Ives (ARPT)*.

(above) **64C it says on the shed plate. Dalry Road, Edinburgh it says in the shed book. One of the Scottish Region's Stanier Cl.5s escapes to England on 13th July 1963. What duty brought No.45360 down to Leeds is unknown but the more than likely answer would be Kingmoor shed borrowing a convenient visiting locomotive for the job. It was returned north shortly afterwards, the number of Holbeck turns over the Settle & Carlisle line making it an easy exercise to get rid of unwanted visitors but a useful cop for enthusiasts. (left) The tablet catcher fitted to the side of 45360's cab. You didn't see too many of those at Holbeck!** *Both Malcolm Foreman.*

(opposite top) **For the sake of some uniformity we'll call this section of the Holbeck sequence 'Visiting Pacifics' and to start the ball rolling we present Gresley A4 No.60012 the one with the longest nameplate! The date is 13th July 1963, a Saturday, and the atrocious looking Pacific was shunting at Holbeck sheds' throat in order to gain entry to the coaling plant.** *Malcolm Foreman.*
(opposite, bottom) **Doncaster A1, No.60157 GREAT EASTERN alongside the water column near the ash plant on one of the roads leading to No.2 shed. Although undated – No.60157 transferred to 36A from 5th April 1959 – we can speculate that this photograph was taken in the early 1960s.** *Brian Ives*

Meanwhile during the previous week from the A4s visit, BR Standard 6P 'Clan' No.72008 CLAN MACLEOD was attending to its fuel requirements at Holbeck's coaling plant on Saturday 6th July 1963. Although not looking its best externally – those steam leaks couldn't have helped its power output – the Kingmoor Pacific had just arrived with the Up service of *THE WAVERLEY* from Carlisle. Besides working over the Settle & Carlisle route and being regular visitors to Leeds, the Kingmoor 'Clans' were regular engines over the West Coast main line to Preston, Liverpool, Manchester, and Crewe. Entering traffic on 14th March 1952 ex-Crewe, No.72008 was allocated to Kingmoor, a shed to which it remained loyal until withdrawn on 16th April 1966 as the last of its class. It was not however the last of the class to remain intact. That dubious accolade went to No.72006 which was cut up at the same Shettleston scrapyard but slightly later. *Malcolm Foreman.*

Another visitor from Doncaster! Peppercorn A1 No.60149 AMADIS looking rather grubby even for January 1964 when this image was recorded. The Pacific hadn't been near works for overhaul since it was released from Doncaster in December 1961 after a General. The A1 was never going to look clean again and as long as nothing drastic happened mechanically, it would remain in traffic. Alas less than six months after this photograph was taken the fifteen-year old locomotive was condemned and then sold to a 'local' scrap yard at Wadsley Bridge. One final word as regards these ex-LNER Pacifics which visited Holbeck was the fact that they could not be turned using either of the two turntables inside the sheds and so had to use one of the triangles with which Leeds was thankfully blessed at that time. Note resident 'Peak' D16 in the background; many of the early numbered 'Peaks' were allocated to Holbeck in that transition period – D11, D12 and D14 to D32 – for instance were all resident by 8th December 1962. Most of those had spent the previous eighteen months working from Neville Hill shed so had been familiar in the city since they were new. *Malcolm Foreman.*

A nice study of by now un-named Kingmoor 'Britannia' No.70048 on the No.1 shed turntable, 18th March 1967. Both of the roundhouses had lost sections of their roofs by this date, this roof was looking rather precarious but it didn't have long to go before steam was banned from the depot and the roundhouses taken down. *K.Groundwater (ARPT)*.

Heaton based A3 No.60051 BLINK BONNY photographed getting some cosmetic attention in the shed yard on an unknown date in 1964 prior to working a rail tour. Coaled, watered, and ready for the 'off' somewhere, the Pacific looks rather magnificent in these two left and right hand poses; those German type smoke deflectors certainly looked the part. *Malcolm Foreman.*

Another special locomotive for a special working! 'Merchant Navy' No.35012 UNITED STATES LINES visited Leeds in 1964 and came to Holbeck for servicing. This might well be 13th June 1964 when the SR Pacific also ran up to Carlisle. Just before this particular foray out of its 'comfort zone' No.35012 had received a Light Intermediate overhaul during the previous March and April which in some way accounted for its superb overall external condition. However, shortly after the 'shopping' the locomotive had been chosen to haul Gresley A4 No.60008 DWIGHT D.EISENHOWER from the locomotive works at Eastleigh to the docks at Southampton from where the A4 was lifted aboard a ship taking it to the United States for preservation at the American Railroad Museum. After that event, No.35012 was itself invited to join the A4 when it was withdrawn but the ignorance and parsimony of the BR authorities came to the fore and the 'Merchant Navy' was sold to a South Wales scrapyard when withdrawn in April 1967. *Malcolm Foreman*.

Note the notice on the right! Note 'Britannia' No.70053 MORAY FIRTH centre stage. It could happen to the best of them! The date is sometime in late September 1962 and the resident Pacific has just been coaled and is now about to have its ash pan emptied, grate cleaned, and have the debris removed from its smokebox. Transferring to 55A in October 1958 from Polmadie – with sister 70054 – No.70053 and its sibling were about to move on again and to yet another region at Crewe North this time. Both would however be back at Holbeck in the future but as regular visitors instead when they moved to Kingmoor shed in January 1966. Oh yes! Another noticeable item is the BR crest on DM D2267 – it is of the correct type with the lion and wheel facing left. *K.Linford (ARPT)*.

During October 1954 a number of A3s were tried over the S&C route between Leeds and Carlisle. They were put to work on the heaviest expresses and sleeper trains. The trials lasted just a week and were deemed to be quite successful. However the Scottish Region authorities did not apparently want to change their carefully planned locomotive rosters concerning the engine workings at Haymarket shed which would have been most affected. Spring forward some six years and the North Eastern Region, which now encompassed the Leeds area sheds, decided to use A3 Pacifics on the S&C route hauling the Anglo-Scottish expresses and the overnight sleepers. Holbeck was the depot chosen to house the A3s which came from far and wide with eight locomotives transferred in to 55A as follows with their dates of residency alongside: 60038 FIRDAUSSI 21st February 1960 to 16th June 1963; 60069 SCEPTRE 20th November 1960 to 11th June 1961; 60070 GLADIATEUR 20th November 1960 to 11th June 1961; 60072 SUNSTAR 20th November 1960 to 16th July 1961; 60077 THE WHITE KNIGHT 21st February 1960 to 11th June 1961; 60080 DICK TURPIN 8th May 1960 to 11th June 1961; 60088 BOOK LAW 8th May 1960 to 16th July 1961; 60092 FAIRWAY 8th May 1960 to 11th June 1961. Some trains were hauled to Glasgow or Edinburgh, others changed engines at Carlisle but the situation only lasted, as can be seen by those dates, until the summer of 1961 although one A3 remained at Holbeck until June 1963. Dieselisation had put paid to the rather unique event. Illustrated in May 1963 is No.60038 the last of the eight. The Pacific was transferred to Neville Hill where it did little if any further work until condemned during the following November. *Malcolm Foreman*.

In amongst the diesels and the snow ploughs! Resident 'Jubilee' No.45593 KOLHAPUR was still earning a living when captured on film on the east side of the shed yard on 26th March 1966. The 4-6-0 worked right to the end at Holbeck when steam was finally banished in September 1967. *A.Ives (ARPT)*.

That's right 66E! This Carstairs based Cl.5 was looking slightly under the weather on 13th July 1963 – note the upper boiler area around the clack valve – and has even been given one of those 'Not to be Moved Fitter at Work' signs. This is 44700 which was one of the BR-built members of the class put into traffic during August 1948 at Perth. Within a few months it was transferred to Carstairs where it remained until withdrawn in July 1966. Yes three years hence from this date. So, in the end the fitter fixed the 4-6-0 and Holbeck sent another Scottish waif back home. *Malcolm Foreman*.

Just look at that 41D shed plate! Stabled in the north-east corner of the shed yard, Thompson B1 No.61370 visits Leeds from Canklow in October 1963. *Malcolm Foreman.*

On 12th March 1961 Holbeck Motive Power Depot was home to this fifty-four years old 25-ton Craven Brothers breakdown crane. The crane was supplied to the North Eastern Railway in 1907 at a cost of £2,498 delivered from the maker's factory at Reddish in Stockport. It was one of three delivered that year under order No.C8153, and all were at the same price. Their NER fleet numbers were CME12, 13, and 14 with CME12 going to Darlington shed, CME13 to York, and CME14 to Gateshead. At the time the trio formed the backbone of the NER breakdown crane fleet and as can be seen were strategically located. At Grouping the LNER numbered them 901637, 901638, and 901639 but by then the last two had been re-located to Middlesbrough and Hull Dairycoates respectively. Our subject here transferred to Sunderland South Dock shed in 1940 and then on 9th January 1961 it was sent to Holbeck for six months by which time it had been renumbered 152 in the BR fleet. In July 1961 No.152 was sent to Dairycoates where on 13th April 1964 it was withdrawn; the Match wagon was numbered 901701 although by the time this image was recorded, it was difficult to discern any legends on the side of the wagon. For the record the second crane – CME13 – became BR 331153 and after withdrawal in March 1971 it became part of the National Collection. The third member of the group was scrapped in 1962. So where was Holbeck's resident breakdown crane whilst No.152 was standing in? RS1004'40 was in works receiving a much needed overhaul. Willesden Cl.5 No.45027 completes the picture. Just as an aside the gentleman in the right foreground is the late Kenneth Gray (The Laird of Hawick). *N.W.Skinner (ARPT)*.

(opposite) **One of Doncaster's 9Fs, No.92170, waits beneath the Holbeck coaling plant in 1963. Turned ready for working back home, the BR Standard would soon be made redundant, put into store in January 1964 and withdrawn the following May some six years and six months old! The coaling plant dates from the LMS modernisation of the depot yard in 1935 when the ash plants were also provided.** *Malcolm Foreman.*

This image from September 1963 shows one of Stourton's newly acquired BR Standard Cl.3s, No.77004, working past the entrance, or throat, to Holbeck depot with a southbound train of empty mineral wagons. In the background a BR Sulzer Type 4 starts across the LNWR Viaduct line with an express for Liverpool (Lime Street). *Malcolm Foreman.*

The tank shed with resident Cl.4s Nos.42052, 42066, and 42055. The date is 11th May 1967 and the roof over the central section of No.1 shed is virtually non-existent. The middle engine is a visitor from Trafford Park and it would be interesting to know the duty and route which brought it to Leeds. *Trevor Ermel*.

Lancaster based LMS Compound No.41196 is made ready for its return home on Saturday 26th April 1958. These 4P 4-4-0s were fast becoming an extinct species and Holbeck's own complement was by now down to a handful with their last examples – 41068, 41094, and 41100 – going for scrap in 1959. Alongside is one of Holbeck's staple 'Jubilees' No.45573 NEWFOUNDLAND carrying the headboard for the Up service of *THE THAMES-CLYDE EXPRESS* which it would be hauling to London later. No.45573 transferred into Holbeck in April 1946 and remained at the depot until withdrawn during the late summer of 1965. *Gordon Turner/GD/ARPT.*

An undated image – thought to be around spring 1963 – captured inside No.1 shed with a pure LMS array of locomotives stabled for the night. From left they were 45661 VERNON from Newton Heath, resident 45597 BARBADOS, resident 42052, resident 43117, an unidentified engine, and 46116 IRISH GUARDSMAN from Kingmoor. All of the engines including the unidentified example but excluding the Manchester engine had been fitted with AWS. Now, if Barrow Hill could arrange such a gathering, complete with the filth, I wonder if it would draw in the crowds!? *Gordon Turner/GD/ARPT.*

Another image from Saturday 26th April 1958 with Ivatt Cl.4 No.43055 our subject; they may have been basic in regard to their appearance, but these ex-LMS 2-6-0s were useful locomotives and Holbeck had a number of them (seventeen) allocated over the years. Four were withdrawn here whilst No.43039 spent the whole of its life at the depot from July 1949 to December 1966 when it was withdrawn. No.43055 arrived in June 1957 along with 43043, 43056, and 43070, and was transferred away in October 1959; one of the shorter residencies. No.43055 ended its career at North Blyth being condemned there in July 1967. Altogether those 17 Ivatt Cl.4s had served Holbeck for a combined total of 78 years and 11 months! *Gordon Turner/GD/ARPT.*

An interesting view of Holbeck and the main line from Nineveh Road bridge in 1964 with steam and diesel locomotives sharing the facilities. *J.W.Armstrong (ARPT)*.

Amongst the diesel locomotives joining Holbeck's allocation in 1958 were this pair of Robert Stephenson & Hawthorn built Drewry Car Co. 0-6-0 diesel-mechanical shunters. D2271 was allocated to Stourton on 14th March 1958 but it went instead to Holbeck where it is seen on 19th April 1958 with sister D2273 which had arrived from Darlington on the day before. Note that both locomotives are wearing the wrong facing new BR crest (*see* **D2267** earlier). **This pair remained at 55A until transfers came into effect as follows: D2271 to Royston 14th May 1967; D2273 to Hammerton Street, September 1966.** *Gordon Turner/GD/ARPT.*

They've always been there it seems! This view of the shed yard on 10th September 1950 shows Stanier Cl.5s, a glimpse of the jib of the depot's breakdown crane RS1004/40, and just near the throat an unidentified Gresley A3 complete with the BRITISH RAILWAYS legend on its tender. So, the question is raised what was that Pacific doing here so early in the decade? There could be lots of answers, the most obvious of which would be that Neville Hill's coaling facility was not available. Do you know? *K.H.Cockerill (ARPT).*

Seen outside No.2 shed on that Sunday in September 1950, Stanier 3P 2-6-2T No.40169 was allocated to Holbeck at the time and had been since the previous March; it was to stay until July 1957 and so keeping a tradition of having at least one of these tank engines allocated since November 1948 – No.40090 – until the last one – No.40140 – was withdrawn from 55A in November 1961. Altogether nine different members of the class had been allocated during that period, with No.40193 having two residences. During the pre-nationalisation period nine of the class had served on and off from March 1938 to July 1947. What duty kept one of these 2-6-2Ts occupied is unknown. A solitary Fowler Class 3 – No.40070 – had also spent most of 1943 at Holbeck. *K.H.Cockerill (ARPT)*.

(*opposite*) **Seen from a train traversing the elevated Viaduct line built by the LNWR in 1882, we get a fleeting glimpse of the shed yard at Holbeck on a typically busy day – Saturday 23rd March 1963 – with main-line diesel locomotives resident amongst the Stanier Class 5s. Note the 40-ton breakdown crane – RS1004 – has been woken from its normal slumbering existence and called upon to help with a lifting job. From this elevation we can see the two huge independent snowploughs allocated to 55A and numbered initially 21 and 22 in the North Eastern Railway scheme but latterly renumbered 900575 and 900576. Weighing just over twenty-seven tons, and of mainly steel construction (the internal walls of each cabin was constructed of timber as was the cabin roof), they dated from 1909 and were stationed at Gateshead engine shed prior to Grouping and into BR days when they were transferred to Holbeck in 1958 when new Gorton-built ploughs arrived at 52A. Standing prow to prow here, they were both ready for renewal and were later superseded by BR-built Nos.900991 and 900992. Finally, the demolition contractor's yard in the foreground holds salvaged items which might one day make the tenants a few bob!** *Malcoln Dunnett (ARPT)*.

(opposite) **Two views of 'Royal Scot' No.46145 THE DUKE OF WELLINGTON'S REGT (WEST RIDING) hauling two of its compatriots – 46109 ROYAL ENGINEER and 46130 THE WEST YORKSHIRE REGIMENT – from Holbeck shed to Farnley Junction shed on Thursday 19th September 1963. All former Holbeck engines, they had been withdrawn in December 1962. The call to Crewe for scrapping saw the most able of the trio steamed to become the haulage as far at Farnley Junction where other motive power was waiting to perform the journey beneath the Pennines and onwards to Cheshire.** *Both Malcolm Foreman.*

In the days when 4-4-0 tender engines were a part of the Holbeck allocation, visiting 4P No.41014 from 19B Sheffield Millhouses is coaled up and ready for its return working on Sunday 10th September 1950. Note that the tender still carries the LMS legend but even almost three years after Nationalisation that was quite normal because BR had thousands of locomotives to put through main works and the cycle of attendance varied with each class. In the event our subject here was withdrawn in May 1952 and then cut up at Derby shortly afterwards. Did the tender ever receive that BR emblem? The chances are fairly slim looking at the dates. When BR came into being, Holbeck, which was then coded 20A under the former LMS scheme, had nineteen 4-4-0 tender engines allocated; of those ten were 4P Compounds the rest were simple 2Ps. *K.H.Cockerill (ARPT).*

They've taken over! They're everywhere! Three Thompson B1s roam the shed yard at Holbeck on 3rd April 1965. Identified are Nos.61250 A. HAROLD BIBBY, 61214 and A.N.OTHER. The reason for the invasion is unknown but there had to be a story behind the infiltration! *N.W.Skinner (ARPT)*.

On the same day another B1 and this Q6 – No.63420 – were stabled at Holbeck. The 0-8-0 note was a Neville Hill engine and therefore we must assume – if that is allowed? – 55H was inaccessible to locomotives and therefore 55A was looking after them. *N.W.Skinner (ARPT)*.

A nice view of the shed yard; 8th September 1963 with a Stanier Cl.5, Kingmoor 'Scot' No.46157 THE ROYAL ARTILLERYMAN and an unidentified 'Jubilee' all resting. The sun is descending and a relative quiet has rested on the depot, for now! But it was a Sunday evening.....'Sing something simple..........' *N.W.Skinner (ARPT)*.

STURDEE at Holbeck in 1967; this was the No.45647's final posting having transferred from Farnley Junction during November 1966. Looking fairly smart for the period – Holbeck tended to clean their 'Jubilees' towards the end – the 6P was kept busy to the end which came in May. *Maurice Burns.*

And to finish off our first visit to Leeds area sheds, we take a look at a couple of former North Eastern Railway roundhouse engine sheds which stood for many years after being abandoned for locomotive purposes. This first example was opened in 1849 by the Leeds & Thirsk Railway, it was one of three roundhouse sheds at this junction and one of two – the other is in fact half a roundhouse also dating from 1849 by the L&TR – which survived into the 21st century as Grade 1 listed. As can be seen here in the 1960s, the premise was being used by a private concern of vessel makers and galvanizers but it was still rail connected. Note the parachute water tank and the pit provided for a pilot engine. *Ken Taylor collection.(NERA).*

And just to the east of that shed was another former NER roundhouse. This was from a later era – opened 1873 – and of a different design. It was being used by the same firm – Thos. Marshall & Son Ltd – but here they manufactured dust bins of the "Mars" brand! Sadly this building was demolished in the 1970s! *Ken Taylor collection.(NERA.*

STOURTON 20B, 55B

1F 0-6-0T No.41661 had spent most of its life working from Kentish Town shed but just a year before the former Midland Railway engine sheds in the West Riding of Yorkshire became part of the North Eastern Region of BR, it was transferred to Stourton. It had not been a direct transfer because it left Kentish Town in July 1951 for Grimesthorpe. Four months later it was sent to Skipton then in April 1952 to Normanton. On 5th May 1957, just five months after Stourton shed gave up its 20B code to become 55B, the six-coupled tank was stabled outside the roundhouse on the stub of track located between the old coal stacks. During BR days Stourton maintained about a half dozen or more of these useful but by now ancient engines for yard work; it had one of the largest allocations of the rapidly diminishing class and only Staveley Barrow Hill had more. Just two years after this scene was recorded, the 0-6-0T met its end but not at Stourton; the deed was done at Goole where it was withdrawn in June 1959. No.41661 had been transferred to 53E just a few days into June 1957. *Clive Allen*.

On the other side of the shed yard on that Sunday in May 1957 – behind the single faced coaling stage – stood 4F No.44454 a visitor from Carnforth. Besides being coaled – the tender tank will be topped up with water prior to departing the shed – the 0-6-0 is turned ready to work back from whence it came. *Clive Allen*.

This gathering of tank engines took place at Stourton on Sunday 10th September 1950 and became a regular weekend occurrence at about this period because access to the roundhouse was becoming rather difficult during certain phases of the rebuilding of the shed. On the extreme right can be seen one of the wooden formers for the pre-cast concrete beams or joists which were mainly cast on site. Anyway, what do we have here amongst the nine 0-6-0 tank engines and one 4F 0-6-0. Immediately identifiable are Nos.41666, 47589, 47443, and 47538, with four more 1Fs including some half-cabs, and another 3F. Miraculously, by the end of the decade all of these tank engines would be gone, either to other depots or for scrap. Stourton was relying on its diesel shunter fleet for its yard duties. The 350 h.p. 0-6-0DE shunters came in small batches: Nos.13294 to 13297 during December 1956 and January 1957; D3454, D3457, and D3458, in June 1957; and D3652 to D3658 during the period March to May 1958 (these were mainly stored and were distributed to other local depots within weeks); one of the diminutive 204 h.p. 0-6-0DMs D2271 also came in March 1958 to complete the rout! *K.H.Cockerill (ARPT).*

We can identify all the locomotives illustrated in this image – if chalked legends are to be believed! The undated view inside the long-completed roundhouse shows from left: WD 2-8-0 No.90605 from Royston; long-time resident 8F No.48703 which had transferred from Holbeck in January 1950 and remained at 55B until January 1967; BR Standard Cl.3 No.77003 which transferred from West Auckland in February 1964 and stayed until withdrawn in December 1966; next we have the shed entrance/exit track; then another BR Cl.3, No.77000 which came from Darlington in May 1964 and remained until withdrawn also in December 1966; and recently arrived resident 8F No.48473 which transferred in from Royston during March 1965 and then returned to 55D in October 1966. We can safely assume that the unknown date is somewhere between March 1965 and October 1966. It is interesting to note that No.48473 has a nicely painted 55B shedplate affixed whereas the two Standards which arrived a year beforehand are bereft any marks of ownership. The two Cl.3s were part of a contingent of ten – half of the class – engines which were drafted in to replace withdrawn 4F 0-6-0s. The control mechanism for the vacuum powered turntable is clearly visible from this angle; note also how tidy the interior of the shed is. *Kevin Hudspith*.

(opposite) **A line-up of Stourton's Standard 3s with only No.77004 identified on 17th July 1965! As already mentioned, Stourton acquired ten of these 2-6-0s with seven arriving in September 1963 from York (3) Thornaby (3) and Dairycoates; three more arrived in early 1964. Of the ten, five were withdrawn at Stourton two transferred to Farnley Junction, another pair went west to Northwich, and No.77002 moved to York.** *N.W.Skinner (ARPT).* *(opposite, bottom)* **Stranger in town! Willesden Cl.5 No.45191 visits Stourton on 19th August 1962. It appears to have been seconded as shed pilot for the day!** *C.J.B.Sanderson (ARPT).*

Eleven of these capable Ivatt Cl.4s have served time at Stourton and No.43038 here was one of the longest serving – September 1957 to May 1964 withdrawal – although not the only one to be withdrawn at 55B. With sister No.43044, they were photographed on the stabling roads behind the coaling stage on Saturday 17th June 1961. *C.J.B.Sanderson (ARPT).*

Besides the diesel shunters already mentioned on page 40, Stourton played host to this one-off special from the Southern Region from 12th July 1952 to 12th June 1956 when it departed and went on loan to Hornsey for three months prior to returning to Norwood Junction where it was eventually withdrawn on 8th August 1959. Arriving at 20B on loan, the 0-6-0 diesel was ex-Three Bridges where it had been for eighteen months. New from Ashford works on 20th February 1950, the Bulleid shunter was numbered 11001. Nothing ever came of it and it was scrapped at Ashford but the longest trial period was the time spent in Leeds on what was then the LMR! Apologies for the less-than-brilliant condition of this image however it's historical important ensures its inclusion. *F.W.Hampson (ARPT)*.

(opposite) Two images to finish off Stourton and representing a near 360 degrees view of the shed yard on 5th May 1957 with 1Fs Nos.41661 and 41797 stabled amongst what is contractors' debris and a dismantled coal stack. The authorisation to rebuild Stourton engine shed roof was sanctioned by the LMS on 28th November 1945 as part of a scheme to renew thirteen roundhouse shed roofs – all former Midland Railway establishments for an estimated expenditure of £350,000. Appears to be a bargain now!

Both John Phillips - Alan Bowman collection.

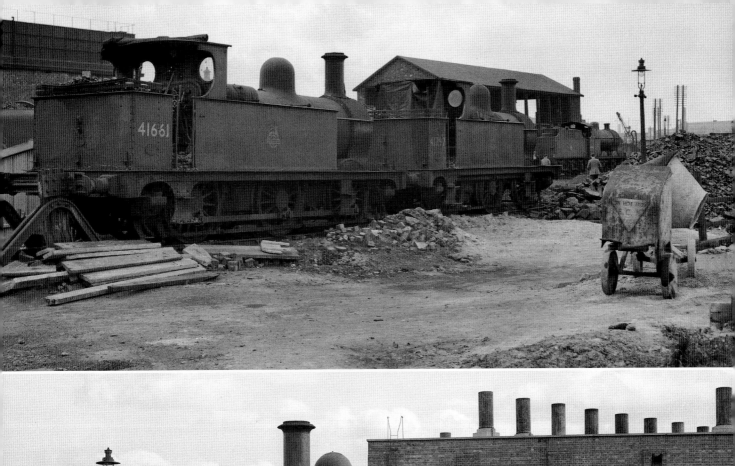

The north-west end of Ardsley engine shed circa 1950 before the large scale rebuilding and modifications were put into play. The northlight roof was a type which became extremely popular with railway companies before 1900 but it often required complete renewal after fifty or more years of service. The Ardsley roof began its operational life in 1893 and although continual maintenance was a factor, by Nationalisation the whole roof not fit for purpose. However, cash-strapped BR could not start work until the summer of 1953; after which a contractor completed the job in just over a year at a cost exceeding £40,000! *K.H.Cockerill (ARPT).*

Not long after the shed roof was completely finished this little gathering became a regular sight at the south-east end of the building. Although undated, it must be approximately 1955 because Ardsley lost its 37A shed code in 1956 and both Thompson B1s were still allocated – for the record 61382 to 61388 began their careers at Ardsley in 1951. One LNER Group Standard tender still wears the BRITISH RAILWAYS legend instigated prior to the adoption of the BR lion-and-wheel emblem. *K.H.Cockerill (ARPT).*

What a nice refreshing change from most 1962 locomotive images. Thompson L1 No.67742 has gone through something of a cleaning process at Ardsley shed during the summer of 1962; shame about those windows but such events were becoming quite rare during this period. The 2-6-4T has just left the coaling plant and is en route to the ash pits. Transferred into Ardsley on 19th November 1961 from Darlington, this L1 was to have something of a short stay at 56B when it was condemned four days before Christmas following that 'refreshing' summer. The engine managed a lifetime mileage of 426,764 miles from being put into traffic on 22nd November 1948. That figure equates to 30,473 miles a year not taking into account time out of traffic at works and awaiting such which accumulated throughout its life into almost a year! *Malcolm Foreman*.

No less than eight of the ten B4 engines built ended their days at Ardsley, most as the LNER became part of British Railways. There was nothing surprising about that fact except the B4 class had all been built for the Great Central Railway by Beyer, Peacock at Gorton Foundry during June and July 1906. Of course they had nothing to do with the West Riding shed until after Grouping when the GC became a major part of the LNER. In 1925 a couple of the class were transferred into Ardsley to work express goods trains but it was 1940 before any more came and then shortly before the LNER ceased to exist they came in numbers! This is No.1482 IMMINGHAM which was one of the 1925 residents but which returned to Doncaster in September 1932. This image was recorded on 24th April 1949 and reveals the 4-6-0 in the green livery it managed to acquire at a March 1947 General overhaul; green was quite rare at Ardsley during that transition period. This second residency at Ardsley began on 11th July 1947 and lasted until called into Gorton in November 1950 after which it was scrapped. *K.H.Cockerill (ARPT)*.

The south-east end of the shed on 3rd April 1965 showing signs of the neglect not only to the external appearance of the locomotive but to the corrugated asbestos and covering of the shed gable! Of course the end was nigh for Ardsley; even with its superior repair facilities it had no place in the BR plan for diesel locomotive care. This view allows us to see along the full length of the south wall of the shed and see the parapet of the Fall Lane overbridge. The 'fire devils' which kept the water columns ice-free every winter would no longer burn coal to produce that welcoming glow on a winter's evening when 'bunking' around the shed was easy under the cover of darkness. At the time Ardsley closed in October 1965, the remaining forty-odd allocated engines were transferred away to numerous depots. As British Railways came into being some ninety locomotives were stationed at Ardsley but successive losses of traffic, and the introduction of main-line diesel locomotives from 1958 saw steam in the area slowly diminish. The B1 here looks ready for the scrapyard but No.61238 LESLIE RUNCIMAN was one of those which survived the closure and was transferred to York on 31st October and then managed to remain in traffic until February 1967. *A.Ives (ARPT).*

Wearing its newly acquired German-style smoke deflectors, No.60080 DICK TURPIN stands outside the repair shop in 1962. Wearing a 56B shed plate at the time, the A3 does not appear to have moved much in recent days nor does it appear to have been cleaned for even longer. This was one of the aforementioned batch sent to Holbeck in May 1960 for work on the S&C. It left 55A on 11th June 1961 and travelled just up the road to Ardsley for a two-year stint working from 56B along with sister No.60070 GLADIATEUR. Both A3s departed Ardsley in June 1963 for Neville Hill but after just six months there the pair moved on to Gateshead but within a year they had been condemned and for some unfathomable reason they both ended up at Drapers scrapyard in Hull albeit during different months of 1964. This image of the eastern aspect affords us a good view of the substantial double-ended repair facility provided by the GNR. *John Pedelty.*

Resident Peppercorn A1 No.60133 POMMERN – minus nameplates – lies condemned and discarded by the old coal stage on 18th July 1965. It had been taken out of traffic on 21st June and was sold for scrap in August to a yard on Tyneside. The coaling stage though made redundant in 1937 remained in situ to the end of the depot's existence as it supported the 200,000 gallon water supply tank. *N.W.Skinner (ARPT).*

Resident B1 No.61013 TOPI looking in a state never envisaged by Edward Thompson but nevertheless the reality of 1960s BR saw most locomotives in this deplorable external condition, named or not! The date is 17th April 1965 when 56B's allocation was down to sixteen WD 2-8-0s, an equal number of B1s of which half carried names, six Ivatt Cl.4 2-6-0s, four Peppercorn A1s, and a couple of V2s. This B1 was amongst the oldest in the class, dating from December 1946. Upon closure of Ardsley it moved on to nearby Wakefield (*see* **Pt.2**) and managed to eke a living until condemned on 6th December 1966 just eight days short of its twentieth birthday! In the left background is the mechanical coaling plant provided by the LNER in 1937 at a cost of £7,437. It had a capacity for 300 tons of coal in twin bunkers. *I.S.Carr (ARPT)*.

A quiet Copley Hill engine shed during an August evening in 1962 with recently acquired Thompson B1 No.61023 HIROLA stabled at the western end of the depot. The rebuilt shed – perhaps more correctly re-roofed – with the work revealed by the new brickwork hiding the steel frame with asbestos cladding, all put up during 1947. The adjacent carriage shed was built of timber, a requisite of the January 1897 estimate which stated that the building would be affected by subsidence from coaling workings. The shed was designed to hold 130 vehicles and its estimated cost amounted to £9,970; it was the first project completed under the Copley Hill expansion. This image was secured from the high ground located between the former GNR main line and the L&NWR main line to the south of the hillock. *John Padelty*.

The N7 class was synonymous to the Great Eastern lines emanating from Stratford shed and its subs. However, Copley Hill saw their presence during the mid-1950s when five of them were allocated for various periods stretching from a week to two years and one month, whilst one of them – 69696 – did two stints between 3rd October 1954 and 4th November 1956! The five locomotives in question were Nos.69691, 69692, 69694, 69695, and 69696. Our subject engine was resident from 3rd October 1954 to 4th November 1956 which was the longest stay. Besides Copley Hill which was late in greeting the class, others – 991E (69613), 996E (69618) and 997E (69619) – went new to Bradford from January 1924 ex-makers' but they had moved on by the summer. In 1942 Bradford was host to eight of the 0-6-2T – 2649, 2650, 2651, 2652, 2654, 2655, 2656, 2658 (69689-69692, 69694-69696, and 69698) – until the last of them left in January 1944. One of the Bradford contingent returned in July 1955 but went away in April of the following year. However, by far the largest concentration took place at Ardsley when from December 1923 it received 990E and then from October 1925 Nos.912, 913, 916, 941, 947, 952, and 968, (69612, 69653-69655, 69660, 60661, 69663, 69667) all new. Then, from 19th November 1927 came new Nos.2600, and 2602 to 2631 (69702, 69704 to 69733). They all moved away to the GE Lines just weeks or months after coming into traffic but Ardsley saw plenty of the class during those heady days of the infant LNER. Finally let's mention those N7s which, just like Copley Hill, came in the mid-50s for stints of a few weeks or a few months: 69691, 69694, 69695, 69696, and No.69698 which came for about eight weeks towards the end of summer 1951. *R.F.Payne (ARPT)*.

A1 No.60117 BOIS ROUSSELL had spent most of its life working from Copley Hill on the expresses to London. This illustration from 1963 shows the engine during its second residency – 15th February 1953 to 6th September 1964 when it was transferred to Ardsley. *Ian W.Coulson.(ARPT).*

A nice view of A1 No.60114 W.P.ALLEN on the yard at the eastern end of the shed in 1951; this Pacific only managed just over two years at Copley Hill, the rest of its life was spent at Doncaster, Grantham or King's Cross. *K.H.Cockerill (ARPT)*.

FARNLEY JUNCTION 25G, 55C

On an undated but wet weekday, and towards the end for the shed, Farnley Junction 'Jubilee' No.45581 BIHAR AND ORISSA heads west past its home with a Newcastle (Central)-Liverpool (Lime Street) express. At the shed throat a 350 h.p. 0-6-0DE shunter is marshalling a BR Standard 9F 2-10-0 onto one of the roads – or perhaps the 9F is marshalling the diesel? During the latter few years of steam on the NE Region, Birkenhead 9Fs, including the former Crosti equipped engines, used to work – double-headed – oil trains from Stanlow refinery to Leeds and the 2-10-0s used to retire to Farnley for servicing once the oil was delivered. The frequency of the oil trains was at least two a day – and night – so the turnover of 9Fs here was quite significant. Add to that, the 9Fs which worked across on ordinary freight turns and Farnley Junction had quite a job keeping the visitors serviced with a contracting local work force. All twelve shed roads are just visible from this aspect which appears to be captured from a signal post and even in the murk of the damp weather we can just make out the single-faced ash plant and the great towering bulk of the coaler located behind the shed. What of the 350 h.p. shunters allocated to 55C? The first two – D3652 and D3653 – arrived new, ex-store at Stourton, on Friday 20th June 1958 and these were joined more than six years later by another pair – D3656 and D3658 – which came from Manningham on 22nd October 1964. All four diesels vacated Farnley Junction for Holbeck at the closure of 55C on 25th November 1966. *Maurice Burns.*

Farnley had a large allocation of these 'Austerity' 2-8-0s which joined BR in their hundreds pre-WW2 when they became available after WD service. No.90726 came to Farnley on 25th November 1950 on transfer from Sowerby Bridge and stayed to the end. Some twenty-odd WDs was the usual allocation up to the early Sixties. No.90726 was withdrawn 12th November 1962 and taken to Darlington works where it was cut up in August 1963. This view from 14th July 1963 shows another aspect at the rear of the shed with a somewhat tidy garden containing outside stores alongside a dedicated flower bed! *C.J.B.Sanderson (ARPT)*.

For most of its operational life from 1935 onwards, the locomotive allocation of Farnley Junction shed remained fairly constant at around fifty locomotives and, from May and June 1936 four of those were Stanier 'Jubilees.' Nos.5703 THUNDERER, 5704 LEVIATHAN, 5705 SEAHORSE, and 5706 EXPRESS arrived new from Crewe but all of them were coupled to Fowler tenders – Nos.3935 (ex-6139), 4246 (ex-6161), 4240 (ex-6155), and 4236 (ex-6153) respectively. The work the engines were expected to do would not require the larger capacity Stanier tenders built for them and so were swapped with the tenders from the 'Royal Scots.' Leeds to Liverpool via Manchester with expresses from Newcastle and Hull were typical of the duties worked amongst others. *(opposite, top)* **Not one of Farnley's clutch but an ex-works engine on a running-in turn from Crewe on 10th September 1950. No.45557 NEW BRUNSWICK was allocated to Kentish Town but had just undergone a Heavy General overhaul – 10th July to 6th September 1950 – at Crewe. The mileage of the turn was typical of the Farnley Junction tender requirements. The 6P is turned and ready for working back to Crewe.** *K.H.Cockerill (ARPT). (opposite)* **One that got away with a Stanier tender. No.45581 BIHAR AND ORISSA was transferred into Farnley Junction on 13th September 1952 from Kingmoor – during a Heavy Intermediate overhaul in actual fact 4th September to 18th October 1952 – and although the works visit would have been the ideal time to change the tenders, it appears to have been overlooked! This is the 6P at Farnley in 1962 wearing the muck and filth livery of that period but still mechanically sound. No.45581 was withdrawn in August 1966 as one of the oldest of her class.** *Ian W.Coulson. (above)* **No.45562 ALBERTA stabled in the shed on 26th March 1966 when Farnley's allocation amounted to about a dozen locomotives. This 'Jubilee' was a late-comer to 55C and arrived in March 1964 from Holbeck returning to 55A in November 1966. Note the lack of a shed plate but the addition of a painted Farnley Jct. legend on the bufferbeam which was not as 'rough' as the 55C painted in place of the shed plate.** *A.Ives (ARPT).*

Sticking with Farnley's 'Jubilees' for a while longer, resident No.45695 MINOTAUR is stabled alongside visiting No.45604 CEYLON from Carnforth in October 1963. This was to be the Farnley engines' final winter of operation, with its withdrawal taking place during the week ending on the 29th day of February 1964. Its lifetime mileage was not very high compared with other 'Jubilees' in other divisions; although only one day younger than sister 45694, their mileage at the end of 1950 was nearly 200,000 miles different with 45695 clocking just 699,225 miles. But 45694 spent most of its life in the Midland Division of the old LMS whereas our subject engine spent all of its life in the former Central Division which had a more intensive service over short distances rather than long distance workings where a 20-mile run would be normal. For the record Farnley Junction was home to some thirty-four of the class during the thirty-odd years the 'Jubilees' were operational; four of whom did two stints at the shed, and one engine managed three residences. Only four of them were withdrawn at Farnley, one in 1963, two in 64' and one in 1966. Their residences stretched from a couple of weeks to more than twenty-six years and everything else in between. The locomotives involved and the dates covered were as follows: 5555 (09-11/44), 45562 (03/64-11/66), 45581 (09/52-08/66W), 5588 (01-03/35), 5591 (01-03/35), 5617 (05-06/37), 5631 (09-11/44), 5642 (05/37-05/40), 45643 (11/63-10/65), 5644 (12/34-03/35), 45646 (09/52-12/63W), 45647 (02/64-11/66), 5661 (05-12/37 & 03/43-07/44), 45671 (11/47-09/48), 45695 (10/52-01/64W), 45697 (02-03/64), 45702 (04/43-09/44 & 12/44-12/50), 5703 (0536-03/43), 45704 (05/36-09/52), 45705 (05/36-06/56), 5706 (06/36-05/43), 5707 (10-11/36 & 02/37-04/43), 45708 (10/36-02/41 & 07/43-09/44 & 12/64-03/64W), 5709 (10/36-10/37), 5710 (10/36-02/37), 5711 (10/36-02/37 & 09/48-09/52), 5712 (10/36-02/37), 5713 (10-12/36), 5714 (10-12/36), 5715 (10/12/36), 5716 (10-12/36), 5724 (03-05/37), 5725 (04/05/37), and 5726 (12/36-05/37). *Malcolm Foreman*.

Besides those Holbeck 'Scots' we have seen being rounded-up, there were others withdrawn at Holbeck which were hauled to Farnley Junction shed for storing until an opportune moment came when two or more could be coupled together to go west! This is No.46103 the late ROYAL SCOTS FUSILIER which was withdrawn at 55C during the week ending 22nd December 1962 after being brought here to await the inevitable; No.46103 arrived with nameplates, works plates and number plate but no 55A shed plate. We are located at the back of the shed where the mechanical coal and ash plants were provided by the LMS during the mid-30s' on the only piece of land suitable. The main line to Huddersfield and Manchester runs past the shed on the right. The WD 2-8-0 behind is No.90726 whilst the tender on the right belongs to 'Crab' No.42766. *John Pedelty*.

Even more 'Royal Scots!' Well one more. No.46145 formerly **THE DUKE OF WELLINGTON'S REGT. (WEST RIDING)** is stored at Farnley Junction in 1963. Again ex-Holbeck and before withdrawal on 8th December 1962; like No.46103 it arrived at 55C with all of its various plates except the shed plate. It was taken to Crewe and cut up at the works there in October 1963. Another ex-Holbeck 'Scot' – albeit a late-comer – which frequented the storage line here was No.46130 **THE WEST YORKSHIRE REGIMENT**. Just beyond the 7P is the coaling plant which was unlike most other such plants from the period. Just beyond the bridge is the LNWR-built enginemens' 'barracks' or lodging house which provided 42 beds for visiting crews. *Malcolm Foreman*.

And they're off! Stanier 8F No.48689, one of Farnley's own, is ready for a run over the Pennine's on an October's evening in 1963. It was usual to move these 'trains of a sensitive nature' at night to lessen the public awareness of so much scrap metal being shifted about the system. By the time this lot reach Mirfield the sun will have dropped below the horizon and a stealthy passage was assured over Standedge. If anything untoward happened en route then Stockport Edgeley shed was designated as a dropping off point – an extra onc or two addcd to 9B's sidings of withdrawn engines would make no difference. The victim's in tow and headed for Crewe were Nos.46161, 46117, and 46109. Each locomotive had a rider who was there to check – using smell and hearing – for the likes of hot boxes or knocking bearings. *Malcolm Foreman.*

A visitor from Crewe! Brand new BR Standard 9F No.92126 is seen on the ash pit road alongside the shed on Saturday 23rd March 1957 after arriving on a running-in turn prior to being allocated to its designated shed at Kettering. Just how many of the Crewe-built 9F 2-10-0s came this way whilst being run-in is an unknown quantity but there were eighty-odd of the class still to be built at Crewe after No.92126 was completed. Just discernible on the extreme right of this image is the bay window of the Shed Foreman's office looking out onto the main line. *F.W.Hampson (ARPT)*.

Visiting from Hull Dairycoates, Thompson B1 No.61255 stables on the shed yard on Saturday 23rd July 1966. In the right distance are the 'barracks'. The shed had been re-roofed in circa 1931 from its original northlight pattern roof and ever since piece-meal repairs had been taking place as witnessed the smoke vents over the road on which the B1 stands. But it was near the end some no-one cared. No.61255 had another year of work until it was condemned and sold for scrap. *N.W.Skinner (ARPT).*

Stockport Edgeley's pride and joy, double-chimney 'Jubilee' No.45596 BAHAMAS stables alongside a filthy and unidentified 350 h.p. 0-6-0DE shunter on Sunday 19th August 1962. *C.J.B.Sanderson (ARPT).*

Mold Junction has sent one of their balanced Stanier 8F 2-8-0s on the 'fitted' job on 14th July 1963. Stanier Moguls, Class 5s and starred 8Fs were regulars on these trains which had been running for decades. No.48090 is turned, coaled and watered awaiting its return to North Wales. Patricroft 'Jubilee' No.45663 JERVIS is likewise awaiting a job which will take it home. *C.J.B.Sanderson (ARPT).*

Just in case you thought all the 'Scots' which visited Farnley junction were en route to scrap yards, we present two images of No.46110 GRENADIER GUARDSMAN on the shed yard on 5th May 1957. The Crewe North 7P was visiting and is ready to work a Newcastle (Central) to Liverpool (Lime St.) express from Leeds after relieving North Eastern motive power. *Both John Phillips-Alan Bowman collection*.

NORMANTON 20D, 55E

The five road engine shed which constituted the covered accommodation at Normanton during BR days was housing a mixture of ex-LMS tank engines and WD 2-8-0s in this 17th July 1966 image. At the Grouping the site contained a polygonal roundhouse dating from 1867 and of Midland Railway and North Eastern Railway origin. The straight shed was built by the Midland in 1882 but for the use of the Lancashire & Yorkshire locomotives using the depot. In order to modernise the depot during the great push for efficiency during the 1930s, the LMS demolished the roundhouse and built a mechanical coaling plant and ash plant approximately in the open area created by the demolition and seen in the right background. This evening view of the shed shows Cl.4 tank No.42149, Ivatt Cl.4 No.43098, and a WD 'Austerity' 2-8-0. *N.W.Skinner (ARPT).*

On that same Sunday in July 1966, this view of the bases of the oil tanks from the erstwhile fuel-oil debacle of 1946 was captured. Four oil tanks were erected along with all the equipment necessary to feed the oil into locomotive tenders. The square building at the end of the site was a boiler house containing two boilers which were used to heat the oil before it was pumped into tenders. Much has been written about that inglorious period of British railway history and that particular chapter. Here we are merely commenting on the aftermath. This area of the shed appears to be somewhere to store locomotives – *see* latter pages – until they are taken away for scrap. However, No.90644 was not withdrawn until 24th June 1967 and was probably awaiting attention for some mechanical problem but look at the cab window which is closed, the usual sign of withdrawal!? The Ivatt Cl.4 No.43116 was withdrawn having succumbed during May. 8F No.48214 was from Westhouses and would return to that depot to be transferred to Colwick in October and then Patricroft in November; its end came in November 1967. Note the tender of the 'Austerity' loaded with some of the better coal available. *N.W.Skinner (ARPT).*

Turning the camera 90 degrees anti-clockwise on the 17th day of July 1966, the shed building comes into view as do two visiting locomotives and resident Q6 No.63426. The 0-8-0 had transferred into 55E from Neville Hill – with sister No.63420 – on 12th June last but it was not staying here too long because on 2nd October it was sent away to Tyne Dock, with 63420. Stanier Class 5 No.45140 is from Springs Branch, Wigan. The 9F is unidentified but was also probably from Lancashire or Cheshire as all the Eastern Region examples had been condemned by this date. From this aspect the shed building really shows-off its Midland influence with the attractive brick inlays on the screen walls. The area around the ash pit and associated lifting plant is pleasantly clear of debris whilst the ash tubs are all empty. Methinks a spot of Sunday overtime had taken place when one of the worse experiences of steam locomotive management has been carried out with some enthusiasm and respect. The vantage point for this and the previous image was the lower levels of the coaling plant which were there for all to use for photography but very few did. *N.W.Skinner (ARPT).*

It's what steam sheds were all about! Steam, smoke, dust, dust, and more dust. You never wore a white shirt although many were the older hands amongst the footplate staff whom used the white shirt as a 'badge of office.' This is Normanton on 26th March 1966 with Dairycoates WD No.90265 yet to be turned for its trip home. On the right is Stourton based Stanier 8F No.48641 adding to the atmosphere. Beyond is a mystery engine shrouded by all that steam. At this period of the BR steam age every single day saw a Hull based WD work over to Stockport with a freight. Likewise Normanton would send one or two of theirs over the Pennines in a virtual conveyor-belt of goods always on the move pre-M62. Such was the volume of traffic plying the former LNWR route between Leeds and Manchester that three tunnel bores were required at Standedge. Of course we can't really mention the Woodhead route or the Summit tunnel route because then we could see how much freight has moved to road transport and why we only have two tunnel bores beneath the Pennines rather than five! Hope valley? *Brian Ives (ARPT).*

Normanton MPD as seen from the Altofts Road bridge on 26th March 1966. Looking north towards York, or Leeds, we have the old Y&NMR main line heading off into the gloom created partly by the depot but also by the coking plants in the area. The shed was still busy as witness the loaded mineral wagons with their various grades of coal for the coaling plant. *A.Ives (ARPT).*

In the days before Normanton became part of the North Eastern Region in January 1957, this is the usual scene welcoming visitors as they walked down the cinder path towards the shed. The date is 21st August 1955 and the row of 1F and 3F tank engines in the distance comprise Nos.41844, 41661, 47335, and 47405. The 4Fs were 44604 with the straight high-sided tender, and 44099; all residents. *K.H.Cockerill (ARPT)*.

The view from where the footpath to the shed led away at ninety degrees from Altofts Road was usually the first glimpse a visiting enthusiast arriving by rail would get. It was less than five minutes walking time from the station. This is where Normanton shed stored their redundant, unwanted, condemned, or withdrawn motive power. This was the view from that road/footpath intersection on Monday 29th August 1960 when 2P No.40630 was laid-up – it was withdrawn on 4th October and taken to Doncaster – having become the last ex-LMS 2P 4-4-0 working from Normanton shed. Sisters Nos.40406 and 40480 which entered the decade working from 20D too had gone in 1952 and 1954 respectively whilst the replacement for the latter, No.40552 was transferred away in June 1955. Two WD 2-8-0s are identified as Nos.90357 and 90021 both residents whilst a pair of rather grotty looking and unidentified B1s are ahead of the 2P. *N.W.Skinner (ARPT).*

Drop of rain, flash of sun, eleven assorted steam locomotives and! A nice image reflects a serious gathering of motive power. Stretching the imagination could take you to the Paint Shop yard at most locomotive works but the left and middle rows of engines are either stored or condemned whereas the right hand line with York V2 No.60932 nearest camera contains operational locomotives which are merely stabled; two 4Fs and a BR Standard complete that line-up. The eagle-eyed amongst you will have noted the Ivatt Cl.4 at the end of the middle row simmering during what appears to be a summer shower, albeit a heavy one. We have no date but we'll throw a few numbers in so that you might get near to sometime in 1963: No.60932 arrived at York on 2nd December 1962 and was condemned there 25th May 1964 and was one of the designated batch of V2s taken to Swindon for scrapping in August 1964. Stanier Cl.3 No.40181 was withdrawn in March 1962 just a few weeks after its arrival from Royston. Note it is still wearing that 55D Royston shed plate and was now merely waiting to be hauled away for scrap. 'Crab' No.42702 was perhaps the 'dark horse' of this bunch in that although looking the worse for wear, it moved on to Ayr in November 1963 – it had arrived at Normanton ex-Bradford Manningham in February 1962 – from where it was eventually withdrawn in January 1966. *Gordon Turner/GD/ARPT.*

Virtually the same location on a rather fine Sunday morning 8th September 1963 with some of the engines from the scene opposite still in situ but also with some extras thrown in for further variety. 4F No.44125 stands where the V2 was stabled, another 4F and a couple of WD 2-8-0s complete the occupation of the line alongside the footpath. The first operational engine shed at Normanton was built in 1850, a joint affair between the North Midland Railway and the York & North Midland Railway and located near the passenger station. It was superseded by the 1867-built roundhouse. The depot was closed from 1st January 1968 the last of the Eastern Region sheds dealing with steam locomotives. Contrast this area of the depot with the same area shown on page 72 but from a different aspect. By July 1966 most of the dross had been moved out and those engines remaining were being condemned weekly it seemed; in 1967 some twenty-six WDs were condemned here alone. Normanton had been home for forty-nine of the class during the ten years that these 'Austerities' had been allocated to the shed. The first examples did not arrive until June 1957 as Normanton became part of the North Eastern Region re-coded to 55E from 20D. Its fifteen limousine-like Stanier 8Fs were sent away to be replaced by a like number of the WD 2-8-0s. *N.W.Skinner (ARPT).*

And to finish off we have this jolly image of Holbeck 'Jubilee' No.45562 ALBERTA visiting Normanton in 1967 after it had become a favourite for specials and rail tours albeit with painted names on backing plates. This view of the immaculate 4-6-0 was taken from the jigger-landing of the coaling plant on a damp but undated day during the final year of 55E's existence. *Maurice Burns*.

Part 2 of Leeds Area Engine Sheds will feature the following depots:
BRADFORD, HUDDERSFIELD, LOW MOOR, MANNINGHAM, MIRFIELD, ROYSTON, SOWERBY BRIDGE, WAKEFIELD, and a few more images of Normanton.

PREFACE

Everyone living in Ireland has a right to health. It is the responsibility of Irish
protect and to deliver that right. The United Nations has made clear that it is not just a right in
itself but is necessary to enjoy our other human rights, to be able, among others, to work or to get
an education.

We stand at a pivotal moment in the development of Irish healthcare. The debate about how we
reform our healthcare system has gone on for decades. There are differing views on how it should be
structured, delivered, funded and made accountable. These are important debates.

But what is missing is a clear, shared understanding of what our health system is designed to
achieve. What are the core principles that drive it? What are its aims, who is it for, what do we
agree is the minimum to which every person who becomes unwell is entitled to? And crucially, how
will our health system fulfil the obligation on Irish governments to deliver the right to the highest
attainable standard of health?

What consensus exists is on the broken nature of our system. One in five of us experience delays
or are denied access to healthcare because we can't afford it. Many find themselves having to
choose between seeing the doctor and paying their bills. People on the margins of Irish society are
more likely to be sick and to find it harder to get the care they need. The Irish health system is not
working for all those who rely on it.

The new Government has made a series of commitments in its Programme for Government on how
it intends to reform our healthcare system. They have promised "access to medical care based on
need, not income". They have promised to "end the unfair, unequal and inefficient two-tier health
system". This pledge to reform presents us with a moment where change is possible.

We cannot squander this opportunity. People are interested in results, not more promises.

The Government must commit to a legal guarantee that no matter who you are, or what you can
afford, you will be taken care of when you get sick. Polling for Amnesty International shows that
people in Ireland overwhelming support such a legal guarantee. They want to know that they can
access healthcare when they need it. They want an end to the fear that comes with getting sick in
Ireland.

Critically, the Government has also committed to requiring all public bodies to be conscious of
equality and human rights principles in their work. Fundamentally, this means putting the patient
at the heart of how we deliver care. But what it will mean in practice, what it means for those
departments and agencies overseeing our health system, has yet to be explained.

This report seeks to outline what the right to health in Ireland looks like. It is a framework. It does
not have all the answers but what it does do is outline the principles, founded in international
human rights law, that we believe must guide and underpin our health system.

Simply put, it requires that when people are sick, they receive the care they need.

Colm O'Gorman

Executive Director
Amnesty International Ireland

INTRODUCTION

Ireland signed the International Covenant on Economic, Social and Cultural Rights (ICESCR) in 1973. However, Ireland has not incorporated the provisions of this Covenant into Irish law. Article 12 of the Covenant provides for the right of everyone to the highest attainable standard of physical and mental health. The right to health is a complex right with many dimensions. This briefing paper, which aims to provide guidance for health policy makers, focuses primarily on the access to healthcare components of the right to health. Health facilities, goods and services have to be accessible to everyone without discrimination. Access must be affordable for all. Where people are required to pay for health-care services, this has to be based on the principle of equity, ensuring that services, whether privately or publicly provided, are affordable for all, including socially disadvantaged groups.[1] However, Irish law and policy do not give adequate attention to the right to health and do not adequately reflect human rights requirements in relation to access to health care.

Amnesty International is working throughout the world – through it's campaign Demand Dignity – to demand accountability for human rights obligations, meaningful access to rights and the active participation of people in the decisions and policies that affect their lives. In Ireland, Amnesty International has been working on economic, social and cultural rights since 2003 and has looked at a number of specific issues, including mental health. Much of our work is done with partner organisations.

International human rights law, as well as the expert guidance of United Nations (UN) treaty monitoring bodies, is a robust framework that can guide policy-makers, clarifying what they are under a legal duty to deliver in terms of social policy, as well as the parameters of that duty. At a time of political and economic change in Ireland, and as various policies on health are debated, human rights law offers a framework that is independent of any political ideology. As the new Government faces into critical policy decisions this paper provides an overview of the right to health, sets out key concerns about the current operation of healthcare in Ireland, and makes a series of recommendations for change in line with Ireland's human rights obligations.

Section 1 provides an overview of the right to health in international law. Section 2 provides a snapshot of health outcomes in Ireland, and Irish law, policy and resources on health. The question of access to healthcare is the focus of Section 3, with a particular stress on the question of economic access. Accountability is critical to ensure rights are adequately protected; section 4 addresses the mechanisms for enforcing the right to health in Ireland.

WHAT IS HEALTHCARE?

Healthcare in Ireland is generally broken down into two types of care: primary and acute. All individuals are entitled to these services. The specific care that they will require will depend on their needs.

SECTION 1: UNDERSTANDING THE RIGHT TO HEALTH

This section will define the right to health in human rights law, setting out the parameters of that right and the nature of the State's obligations.

1.1 THE RIGHT TO THE HIGHEST ATTAINABLE STANDARD OF PHYSICAL AND MENTAL HEALTH

Article 12 of the International Covenant on Economic, Social and Cultural Rights (ICESCR) recognises the "right of everyone to the enjoyment of the highest attainable standard of physical and mental health".[2] The exact parameters of the right have been further developed over time.

It is important to note that the right to health is not the right to be healthy – no one can have perfect health all the time.[3] In 2000, the Committee on Economic, Social and Cultural Rights (CESCR) issued an expert commentary clarifying what the right to health entails.[4] This commentary explains that the right to health is to be understood as a framework of freedoms and entitlements. The freedoms include the right to control one's health and body and to be free from, for example, non-consensual medical treatment. Entitlements include the right to "...a system of health protection which provides equality of opportunity for people to enjoy the highest attainable level of health".[5]

> (a) Right to health facilities, goods and services, and the underlying determinants of health

The right to health is an inclusive right which includes not only timely and appropriate healthcare but also "the underlying determinants of health, such as access to safe and potable water and adequate sanitation, an adequate supply of safe food, nutrition and housing, healthy occupational and environmental conditions, and access to health-related education and information, including on sexual and reproductive health". Human rights law sets out criteria for determining whether the underlying determinants of health or health facilities and services are compatible with human rights principles. The right to health thus contains the following "interrelated and essential" elements:

- *Availability.* Health facilities, goods and services must be available in sufficient quantity within the country. This includes, for example, hospitals, clinics, trained health workers, essential medicines, preventive public health strategies and health promotion as well as underlying determinants, such as safe drinking water and adequate sanitation facilities.

- *Accessibility.* Health facilities, goods and services must be accessible to everyone without discrimination based on:
    - a policy of non-discrimination in law and in practice;
    - physical accessibility (including for marginalized people including people with disabilities;
    - economic accessibility (affordability) whether privately or publicly provided;
    - accessibility of information, including the right to seek, receive and impart information, consistent with confidentiality of personal data.

- *Acceptability.* All health facilities, goods and services must be respectful of medical ethics and culturally appropriate.

- *Quality.* Health facilities, goods and services must also be scientifically and medically appropriate and of good quality. This requires, among other things, that there be skilled medical staff, scientifically approved drugs and hospital equipment and adequate sanitation.

The obligation under human rights law is to the highest attainable standard of physical and mental health. The health facilities, goods and services to which government is obliged to ensure equal access include basic preventative, curative, rehabilitative health services and health education; regular screening programmes; appropriate treatment of prevalent diseases, illnesses, injuries and disabilities; and appropriate mental health treatment and care.[6]

Critical to the right to health is also the right to participate in all health-related decision-making at community, national and international levels. In order to participate properly, people also need to enjoy the right to receive and impart information.

1.2 THE NATURE OF STATE OBLIGATIONS ON THE RIGHT TO HEALTH

The International Covenant on Economic, Social and Cultural Rights is a legally binding agreement between States and places clear legal obligations on those States. Treaty monitoring bodies have recognised that human rights, including the right to health, place three types of obligations on States: to respect, to protect and to fulfil. The obligation to **respect** places a duty on States to refrain from interfering directly or indirectly with the enjoyment of the right to health. The obligation to **protect** means that States must prevent third parties from interfering with the enjoyment of the right to health. The obligation to **fulfil** requires States to adopt necessary measures, including legislative, administrative and budgetary measures, to ensure the full realisation of the right to health.

(a) Right to health violations

Violations of the right to health can occur if governments do not respect, protect and fulfil the right to the highest attainable standard of health. Violations occur when governments:

- Deny access to health facilities, goods and services to particular individuals or groups as a result of discrimination;

- Deliberately refuse to give information, or give misleading information that may be vital to health protection or treatment;

- Fail to take steps to improve the underlying determinants of health;

- Do not take effective and adequate action to reduce infant and maternal mortality rates;

- Fail to ensure healthy workplace and natural environments;

- Neglect to set up systems to prevent, treat and control disease.[7]

The right to health cannot be realised in a vacuum. It is intrinsically linked to the right to an adequate standard of living, including food and adequate housing, the rights to life, work, education, non-discrimination, equality, the prohibition against torture, privacy, access to information, and the freedoms of association, assembly and movement.

4

(b) Progressive realisation and resource availability

International human rights law recognises that certain elements of economic, social and cultural rights – including the right to health – may not become reality overnight, but will take some time to realise, depending on the availability of resources. However, states are required to use maximum available resources to progressively realise the right to health. In human rights law the concept of progressive realisation encompasses an obligation on the state to move as expeditiously as possible towards the full realisation of the right. The Committee on Economic, Social and Cultural Rights (CESCR) has detailed the obligation on states that are party to the Covenant to follow a course of action that would achieve fulfilment of the rights in the Covenant in the shortest possible period of time. The level of fulfilment of any right will be determined by the economic conditions prevailing in a particular state.[8]

How a government allocates its resources provides a strong indication of a government's policy priorities. Where violations of economic, social and cultural rights occur, they are not simply a matter of inadequate resources, but a result of policy decisions.[10] Where states seek to justify a violation of economic, social or cultural rights due to a lack of financial, technical or human resources, it is necessary to look at whether the state has given "sufficient priority to human rights when setting budgets".[11] This requirement to take their human rights obligations into consideration when setting budgets (the most visible process of resource allocation by government), has been identified as one of the key features of a health system necessary to fulfil the right to health. Former UN Special Rapporteur on the Right to Health, Paul Hunt, in his report to the UN Human Rights Council in January 2008 sets out the obligations on member states to have a health system where the allocation of resources is decided on in a transparent and fair manner, considering the most vulnerable and not just the powerful interest groups.[12] Both the overall level of resources, and the allocation of those resources, including equality of funding, can be relevant. The CESCR has noted that "health resource allocation can lead to discrimination that may not be overt."[13] For example, the UN Special Rapporteur's 2005 report noted in the case of mental health services: "Inappropriate resource allocation can lead to inadvertent discrimination."[14] The allocation of resources is also frequently used by states to make choices *within* a particular policy area e.g. direct grant payments versus subsidising cost to the individual for a particular service.

In any assessment of whether a state is meeting its obligations of progressive realisation, there is a strong presumption that going backwards in the realisation of the right to health would constitute a violation of the right to health.[17] If any deliberately retrogressive measures are taken, then the State has the obligation to prove that they have been introduced after the most careful consideration of all alternatives and that they are duly justified by reference to the totality of the rights and in the context of the full use of state's maximum available resources.[18]

Regardless of the level of resources in question, implementation of the right to health must always be on the basis of non-discrimination, and there must be a clear plan in place as to how the State will fulfil this right over time.[19] Measurement of progressive realisation requires the use of appropriate indicators and benchmarks.[20] Otherwise there is no way of knowing whether or not the state is improving its health system. Indicators must be disaggregated on relevant grounds that will allow the state to know whether or not the right to health of vulnerable groups is being adequately addressed.

It is also critical to monitor resources to ensure that resources allocated are delivering upon the area of rights which they address e.g. health. Analysis of budgets is a critical tool in assessing governments' performance: "[b]udget analysis can often pinpoint inadequacies in expenditure, misdirection of funds or a 'misfit' of expenditures relative to the government's stated human rights commitments."[15] Similarly, such analysis can help identify where funds have been blocked or where they have "leaked" (i.e., disappeared) as they are disbursed from one level of government to another."[16]

(c) Immediate obligations

While human rights law provide for the progressive realisation of the right to health, the law also places a number of immediate obligations on states, which are not subject to progressive realisation and must be immediately implemented.

States that are party to the ICESCR must take deliberate, concrete and targeted steps, as "expeditiously and effectively as possible", towards fulfilling the right of everyone to the highest attainable standard of health. The adoption of legislative and other measures are steps to the realisation of any right.[21] Any such steps must be deliberate, concrete and targeted towards the full realisation of the right to health. This duty to "take steps" is an immediate obligation. The concept of progressive realisation of rights does not justify government inaction on the grounds that a state has not reached a certain level of economic development. This requires, at a minimum, that states adopt a national strategy to ensure to all the enjoyment of the right to health, based on human rights principles that define the objectives of that strategy.[22]

Another immediate obligation is the state's duty to prioritise "minimum core obligations" i.e. minimum essential levels of each of the rights. Under the right to health, core obligations include essential primary healthcare; access to health facilities, goods and services on a non-discriminatory basis, especially for vulnerable or marginalized groups, and essential drugs, as from time to time defined under the WHO Action Programme on Essential Drugs.[23]

The duty not to discriminate (see below) is also an immediate obligation. The adoption of laws, policies or practices that have a direct or indirect discriminatory impact on the ability of people to realise their rights amounts to a human rights violation.

The duty to prioritise the most vulnerable is also an immediate obligation. The state should actively reach out to marginalised and excluded people, who face the greatest barriers in realising their rights, and they should be given "first call" when allocating resources.[24]

(d) Equality and non-discrimination

The principle of non-discrimination is at the core of the international human rights system.[25] Discrimination can be direct or indirect. Direct discrimination is unfavourable treatment that is, on the face of it, based on a prohibited ground. Indirect discrimination occurs where a law, policy or practice appears neutral but results in a disproportionate disadvantage or negative impact on the exercise of rights by a particular group. Discrimination, whether intentional or not, can have wide-ranging negative impacts in the context of the right to health, including preventing certain individuals and groups from accessing or obtaining necessary healthcare and preventing or impeding their participation in development of health policy.[26]

The Committee on Economic, Social and Cultural Rights has clarified that discrimination is prohibited on "grounds of race, colour, sex, language, religion, political or other opinion, national or social origin, property, birth, physical or mental disability, health status (including HIV/AIDS), sexual orientation and civil political, social or other status, which has the intention or effect of nullifying or impairing the equal enjoyment or exercise of the right to health".[27] The Committee has also recently affirmed that an individual's social and economic situation is a prohibited ground for discrimination.[28] That someone is living in poverty, for example, is not a permitted reason to discriminate against him or her.

The state must not only refrain from discriminating itself, but must also protect against discrimination by non-state agents, such as private healthcare providers. According to the Committee on Economic, Social and Cultural Rights, "States parties must therefore adopt measures, which should include legislation, to ensure that individuals and entities in the private sphere do not discriminate on prohibited grounds."[29] For example, a private hospital cannot refuse to treat an individual on the basis of their gender or ethnicity. While a legal prohibition on discrimination by private actors is important, legislation alone is rarely sufficient. Legislation must be implemented effectively, and additional measures such as awareness-raising are also required. Different treatment is permitted, and does not constitute discrimination, "if the criteria for such differentiation are reasonable and objective and if the aim is to achieve a purpose which is legitimate..."[30]

States must adopt and implement a national health strategy 'with particular attention to all vulnerable or marginalised groups' and that 'respects the principle of non-discrimination'.[31] This requires that any healthcare provision take account of the particular needs of marginalised groups, but also that any care provided is culturally appropriate to that group. Culturally appropriate healthcare provision involves a range of interventions including ensuring availability of interpreter services, culturally and linguistically appropriate health education materials and training to enhance service providers' knowledge of the relationship between socio-cultural factors and health.

1.3 OBLIGATION OF ACCOUNTABILITY

A fundamental requirement of human rights is that the State is accountable. An accountability procedure is a mechanism whereby duty-bearers (the state) are answerable for their actions. Broadly speaking, there are four categories of accountability mechanism:

- Judicial, e.g. judicial review of executive acts and omissions;

- Quasi-judicial, e.g. Ombudsman institutions, international human rights treaty-bodies;

- Administrative, e.g. the preparation, publication and scrutiny of human rights impact assessments;

- Political, e.g. parliamentary processes.[32]

7

SECTION 2: HEALTH AND HEALTHCARE IN IRELAND

This section will provide a brief overview of health in Ireland. It is not a comprehensive analysis but is offered as context for the subsequent focus on access to healthcare.

2.1 HEALTH IN IRELAND

According to recent surveys, the average life expectancy at birth in Ireland is 80 years; two years more than the EU average.[33] The population's neonatal mortality rate was just 3 per 1,000 births, slightly above the EU average.[34] The principal causes of death are circulatory diseases and cancers.[35] While these macro-level indicators are valuable, they do not offer any information about health inequalities within the population. There are significant inconsistencies in the individual health experience across the population. For example, the members of the Traveller community have "substantially higher rates of ill-health affecting them on a day to day basis than is demonstrated in the comparator populations."[36] Life expectancy at birth for a male traveller is 15.1 years less than men in the general population.[37] Similarly, the Traveller community has higher infant mortality rates than the general population.[38]

A notable issue in health inequality is the degree to which health status is determined by individual socio-economic status.[39] Data from the EU survey on Income and Living Conditions in Ireland revealed significant inequalities in health and illness between socio-economic groups. 85% of those who were 'non-poor' reported good or very good health, whereas this was true of only 66% of those experiencing income poverty.[40] Furthermore, 47% of those living in consistent poverty reported having a chronic illness compared with 23% of the general population.[41] This inter-relationship between poverty and ill-health is also reflected from data in 2009 which shows that individuals with chronic illness, health problems or who perceived themselves to have a poorer health status were more likely to be at risk of poverty.[42] This data reflects the fact that people living in poverty are more likely to have poor health, and people with poor health are more likely to experience poverty. This is particularly critical when we consider that an individual's economic status and ability to pay are critical to their ability to access healthcare in Ireland (see below). Efforts to address these problems are contentious areas of public debate, attracting significant political interest and various efforts at healthcare reform.

2.2 IRISH LAW AND POLICY AND RESOURCES ON THE RIGHT TO HEALTH

Ireland is a party to ICESCR and has undertaken to realise the right to the highest attainable standard of health. However, there is no right to health in Irish Constitutional or statutory provision (see section four). This absence does not mean that Ireland is, per se, not delivering upon the right to health. While the Irish national health strategy, Quality and Fairness: A Health System for You[43] (hereafter Quality and Fairness) includes some principles relevant to human rights, such as equity and accountability, it does not systematically integrate human rights. Indeed the UN has recommended that the health strategy should "integrate a human rights framework", specifically "in line with the principles of non discrimination and equal access to healthcare".[44]

There is insufficient monitoring and tracking of data within the Irish healthcare system to measure implementation of, for example, the national health strategy. Despite annual reporting commitments within Quality and Fairness there has not been an Action Plan Progress Report on the strategy published since 2007, which was based on 2006 activities. The Health Service Executive (HSE)[45] publishes Performance Reports to monitor progress against its objectives and commitments, including reporting on levels of expenditure and levels of care provided. However, the Expert Group on Resource Allocation and Financing in the Health Sector (hereafter the Expert Group)[46] has stated that "some information systems within the Irish health sector are presently not 'fit for purpose'. This became evident to the Expert Group as it discovered that basic data on, for example, the operation of the public and private health systems could only be obtained with great effort."[47]

In addition to the law and policy underpinning the health system, a fundamental question is the level of resources in any area and how they are allocated. State expenditure on health in Ireland has increased substantially as a proportion of GDP since 2000.[48] In 2008, Irish health expenditure as a percentage of GDP was 8.7%[49], equating to €18.829bn.[50] However, Ireland's expenditure on health as a percentage of GDP is slightly below the OECD average of 9.0%.[51] It is also important to note that some items of social spending are included within health expenditure in Ireland – for example spending on community welfare services – making spending comparisons difficult. Approximately, 20% of health expenditure is actually social expenditure.[52] This is not to suggest that there is a clear line from increased expenditure to better outcomes, including fulfilment of the state's human rights obligations, but to give contextual information for further analysis. It is also not merely a question of the total level of resources in a given area but how those resources are allocated.

A further significant issue is the level of private expenditure on health in Ireland.[53] In 2008, €18.839bn of total expenditure was made up of €15.172bn in total public health gross expenditure, €1.262bn in private insurance spending, €2.289bn of out-of-pocket expenditure (i.e., people paying health service providers directly for services e.g. GP fees), and €116 million on private investment.[54] Overall spending rose in 2009 to €19.7bn. Recent analysis suggests that despite the high levels of private insurance coverage in Ireland, only 7% of total health spending in Ireland can be attributed to the private health insurance companies.[55]

Total Health Expenditure

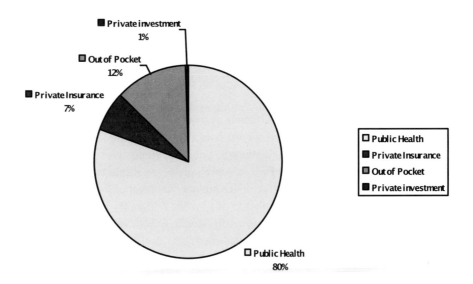

9

The question of the level of out-of-pocket expenditure is particularly relevant where the ability to meet those costs impacts on access to healthcare. This issue, and other barriers to access to healthcare, are discussed in section three.

Resource allocations do not always follow the agreed policies and strategies of the state. The Expert Group found that even where Irish health policies include important principles such as equity and accountability, resources are not fully aligned to support the implementation.[56] They also stated that "the current [healthcare] financing system in Ireland lacks transparency, [and] gives rise to serious inequities in access to care".[57] In October 2010 the government indicated it was giving "detailed consideration" to the report of the Expert Group, which includes a number of recommendations on how resources can be allocated to increase equity of access to healthcare. At time of publication, the Government elected following an election in February 2010 has not announced its intentions with regard to the report. The focus of the report on equity is particularly relevant to the human rights obligations of equal access given the note of the UN Special Rapporteur on the right to health that "[t]here is no universally accepted definition of equity, but one sound definition is 'equal access to healthcare according to need'."[58]

One of the critical features of Irish healthcare is the relationship between public and private provision. Despite the fact that the majority of European countries practice some form of mix in the public/private provision of healthcare, what is quite exceptional is the fact that in Ireland a substantial amount of private healthcare takes place *within* the state-funded public hospital infrastructure.[59] They are not entirely separate systems. As well as dedicated private hospitals and medical professionals the private provision of health services is integrated into the public health system. For example, under the National Health Strategy, public hospitals are mandated at policy level to ensure that 20% of hospital beds are reserved for private patients.[60] Hospital consultants receive a salary for public patients, while receiving fees for private patients. The majority (75%) of hospital consultants' contracts with the HSE stipulate that 20% of their practice should be allocated to private patients.[61] The remaining (25%) of consultants have contracts where they work entirely in the public health system. Similarly GPs, have both private and public patients. The previous government themselves acknowledged that this situation has contributed to unacceptably long waiting lists for public patients.[62] Regardless of how the healthcare system is arranged, the obligation on Ireland is to ensure that everyone can access healthcare services. The critical question is how the implementation and operation of those services impacts on individuals access.

2.3 RESPONSIBILITY FOR THE DELIVERY OF HEALTHCARE IN IRELAND

Health policy, legislation and strategic management are the responsibility of the Department of Health and Children under the control of the Minister for Health and Children. The HSE is responsible for executing policy, administration and management of services. The HSE is accountable to the Department of Health and Children, primarily through the Minister.[63] This does not change or reduce the legal responsibility of the state for its human rights obligations but has implications in practice. There is a significant gap in accountability in that, while the HSE is essentially accountable to the government for delivery of services and balancing the budget, the level of detail provided in performance reports is not sufficient to ensure accountability for outcomes.[64] The Government has indicated that the Health Service Executive will cease to exist over time, with the functions deployed elsewhere.[65] It is critical that, whatever the nature of the infrastructural arrangements put in place, sufficient accountability is exercised by Government over the delivery of healthcare and the wider components of the right to health.

SECTION 3: ACCESS TO HEALTHCARE IN IRELAND

The right to health is multi-dimensional. Access to healthcare is a critical component and includes non-discrimination, physical accessibility, economic accessibility (affordability), and access to information about health issues. This section will outline some of the overall provisions for access within the Irish healthcare system, with a particular focus on economic access.

3.1 IRISH HEALTH POLICY ON ACCESS

Delivering healthcare in Ireland [66]

Primary care in Ireland is delivered by private GPs, who are gatekeepers for hospital treatment, providing letters of referral to acute care for their patients. GPs are located in the community in single/multi-person practices although the trend for single-handed practices is declining and primary care teams (PCTs) are being created gradually throughout the country in line with national policy.

Primary, continuing and community care is also provided by a range of other health professionals including community-based pharmacists (private practitioners), public health nurses, social workers, health-care assistants, home helps, midwives, occupational therapists, physiotherapists, etc. In addition, there are public and private facilities that provide non-acute long-term health care. Public long-stay units include geriatric hospitals and homes, district and community hospitals, and HSE welfare homes.

Acute health-care services are delivered in HSE public, voluntary public and private hospitals. There are 34 HSE hospitals and 18 voluntary hospitals. Although the total number of beds in acute public hospitals has not grown substantially in recent years, the composition of these beds has changed significantly, with a shift from inpatient beds to day beds. The acute public hospital sector is currently undergoing substantial reconfiguration, involving the concentration of acute services in regional hospitals, with local hospitals focusing on elective services. There are approximately 20 purely private hospitals (including private psychiatric hospitals), which receive no direct state grant funding. The private hospitals operate in parallel to the public hospitals but there are some services that are not available in the private sector (e.g. complex treatments such as liver transplants).

In principle, people in Ireland are generally expected to cover the cost of their own healthcare. The Health Act of 1970 established that individuals are responsible for the costs of their own healthcare except in cases where this would cause that individual "undue hardship". People pay for their own healthcare through

11

direct payment for services and goods e.g. GP visits. For more than 50% of the population payment for some services is covered by private medical insurance. However, private medical insurance does not cover all elements of healthcare – for example GP visits are not as a rule covered by insurance and individuals must pay a fee per visit. While the majority of the population pays directly or via insurance for healthcare, the State also provides for some free or subsidised access for individuals who would be assessed as suffering undue hardship of they had to pay for healthcare (discussed further below). The State provides some specific healthcare services regardless of ability to pay, for example maternity and infant care services.[67]

The 2001 national health strategy, *Quality and Fairness*[68], was intended to indicate "the point where a Government committed to equity, accountability, fairness and people-centeredness embedded these principles in the way we plan and deliver Ireland's health services."[69] The strategy set out how the health needs of particular groups would be addressed including children, people with disabilities, older people, people with mental health problems, women, men, and people experiencing other health inequalities.

One of the most significant issues with regard to access to healthcare is the limited capacity of the public healthcare system to meet the needs of the population.[70] This has resulted in the persistent issue of public hospital waiting lists to access healthcare. *Quality and Fairness* adopted a number of strategies aimed at increasing the number of hospital beds available to public patients through the use of existing resources in private hospitals.[71] This is explored further in section 3.3(c).

3.2 ACCESS TO HEALTHCARE FOR SPECIFIC GROUPS, INCLUDING KEY CHALLENGES.

Human rights law requires that healthcare services must meet the needs of individual sectors of the population. In the first instance this means that these services be made available without discrimination.[72] It also requires the state to take proactive measures to provide for vulnerable and marginalised groups, for example through specific strategies and health programmes.[73] This includes access to essential primary healthcare at a minimum,[74] an equitable distribution of facilities, goods and services[75]; and adoption and implementation of a national health strategy 'with particular attention to all vulnerable or marginalised groups' that 'respects the principle of non-discrimination'.[76] In addition to *Quality and Fairness* there are a number of national specialised strategies. These include the primary healthcare strategy,[77] several concerning vulnerable groups such as the national women's health strategy,[78] Traveller health,[79] and specific 'crisis' targets, such as alcohol and drug use.[80] Specific health areas are also provided for, such as suicide prevention, chronic diseases, and mental health.[81]

Despite these strategies, there are undeniable discrepancies in access to healthcare and in health outcomes across different groups. Access to healthcare can vary according to what part of the country a person lives in as well as the nature of their medical problems. There are significant barriers in the physical access to services for people with disabilities and older people, mainly due to lack of transport.[82] Access to mental health services is not even available at the minimum standard across much of the country.[83] The National Women's Council of Ireland has criticised the lack of gender mainstreaming in Irish healthcare policy, planning and services, which fail to adequately reflect the specific health needs of women.

12

Barriers in accessing healthcare have been noted within those populations experiencing poorer health outcomes. While the significantly lower life expectancy within the Traveller community (described above) is linked to multiple other factors around the social determinants of health, barriers to accessing healthcare were specifically identified. Respondents to the All Ireland Traveller Health study cited waiting lists (62.7%) and a lack of information (37.3%) as barriers to accessing healthcare.[84] Another study highlighted difficulties in completing Medical Card renewal forms due to high illiteracy levels within the community, which consequently acts as a barrier to accessing primary healthcare.[85] This data on barriers to access to healthcare is not available for the general population but would be valuable in any policy analysis and, ultimately, ensuring that the health system is designed and operates in a way to ensure accessibility.

Similarly there are concerns around access to healthcare for the migrant population in Ireland. There are specific concerns around access of migrants to healthcare in light of the fact that entitlement to health services in Ireland is primarily based on residency and means.[86] People who meet the requirement of ordinary residence are entitled to access state-subsidised healthcare services, including for example, the Medical Card system. Both regular and irregular migrants who do not meet this requirement may be asked to meet the full charges for a healthcare service. One of the most problematic issues in meeting this residence requirement is the Habitual Residence Condition, which requires that a person have a proven link with Ireland determined by a number of factors including length of residence period in Ireland,[87] in order to secure welfare entitlements. As a consequence, many migrants are excluded from accessing state services, including health services, other than emergency medical treatment, until they meet this condition.[88] Recent evidence suggests a multiplicity of barriers for migrants and ethnic minority groups in accessing healthcare services, including entitlement to free services.[89]

DEMOGRAPHY OF POVERTY IN IRELAND

Poverty affects multiple sectors of the population in Ireland. The "at risk of poverty" rate is lower when the head of the household is male. Female-headed households have, on average, lower net disposable household incomes.[90] The 2008 Report on the Consultation for the National Action Plan against Poverty and Social Exclusion,[91] from the Office of Social Inclusion, specifically identified individuals with mental health problems, Travellers, migrant workers, asylum seekers and refugees as groups at particular risk of poverty. While individual groups face specific challenges in accessing healthcare, poverty is an important lens to use in any policy analysis, as it will reflect the experiences of multiple groups.

3.3 ECONOMIC ACCESS TO HEALTHCARE – A CRITICAL BARRIER IN IRELAND

In addition to specific issues for particular groups within the population, as discussed above, there are significant concerns around the question of economic access. This is the focus of this policy briefing. Fundamentally, government must ensure that cost is not a barrier to individuals accessing healthcare services. The Committee on Economic, Social and Cultural Rights has made clear that "payment for healthcare services... has to be based on the principle of equity, ensuring that these services whether privately or publicly provided, are affordable for all, including socially disadvantaged groups. Equity demands that poorer households should not be disproportionately burdened with health expenses as compared to richer households."[92] If a health system is accessible to the wealthy but not to those living in poverty then the State may be held accountable and ordered to rectify this.[93]

Ireland is obliged to respect the right to health by not discriminating against individuals, including denying or limiting access to healthcare.[94] It must protect the right to health by adopting legislation or other measures to ensure equal access to healthcare; this would include measures to ensure that privatisation of the health sector does not constitute an obstacle to the accessibility of healthcare.[95] Finally, Ireland is obliged to fulfil the right to health by providing a public, private or mixed health insurance system that is affordable for all.[96] A violation of the obligation to fulfil would occur where the failure to direct maximum available resources resulted in the non-enjoyment of the right to health for individuals or groups, particularly vulnerable or marginalised sectors of the population.[97]

(a) Irish policy on economic access

This section focuses on where cost acts as a barrier to individuals accessing healthcare services in Ireland. In Ireland, the default position is that individuals are responsible for the costs of their own care except where this would cause that individual 'undue hardship'. As noted above, this was established by the 1970 Health Act which introduced the Medical Card system entitling free access to health services within the public system.[98] Determination of eligibility for a Medical Card is the responsibility of the Health Service Executive (HSE) and there are three primary means of determining eligibility: means test, discretionary assessment and EU Entitlement. Both the means test and the discretionary assessment are based on the concept of avoiding 'undue hardship', to an individual if they had to pay their own medical costs. EU entitlement is the result of agreements with EU countries on access to healthcare. The primary way the State assesses the likelihood of 'undue hardship' is through a means test of income. Income guidelines are used to establish eligibility[99] and are intended to ensure that individuals below a certain level of income have access to healthcare without cost. In relation to hospital fees individuals with a Medical Card have cost-free access to acute healthcare. Non-Medical Card holders are liable for statutory in-patient and outpatient charges for public care in public hospitals.[100]

Four broad entitlement groups can be identified in terms of payment for medical services;

1. Approximately 39.5% of the population hold either a full **Medical Card or GP visit card, and have no private health insurance**.[101] The Medical Card entitles the holder and dependents to free access to public hospital services, GP and prescription care[102] and a range of other benefits.[103] The GP visit card entitles the holder to free access to GP consultations.[104] A separate income threshold applies for persons over 70 years of age.[105]

2. Approximately 49% of the population is in possession of **private health insurance**.[106] While the level of healthcare coverage depends on the insurance package purchased, most private health insurance covers costs related to hospital care, not primary care.

3. Approximately 4% of the population has **dual cover** of both a Medical Card and private health insurance.[107]

4. **Non-covered** – 19% of people have neither Medical Card nor private health insurance.[108] Individuals without a Medical Card or GP Visit Card are required to pay for GP visits at the point of use; fees are not set or regulated in any way, but payments can be reclaimed against taxation.[109] Non-Medical Card holders are also liable for statutory in-patient and out-patient care in public hospitals. The standard daily charge for in-patient care is €75, up to an annual maximum of €750. Emergency department visits are free, if referred by a GP, otherwise €100.[110]

(b) Key challenges in ensuring economic access to healthcare in Ireland

The fact that healthcare in Ireland is provided through both public and private means does not change or reduce the obligations on the government to ensure that cost does not act as a barrier to people accessing healthcare. Access to both primary and acute (encompassing secondary and tertiary)[111] healthcare services must be analysed in terms of the affordability to the individual. Four elements are key in assessing economic access to healthcare for people in Ireland. These are affordability of primary care, affordability of acute care, waiting time for care based on ability to pay, and how the government allocates resources to ensure that health care is affordable and accessible for everyone.

- Access to Primary Care[112]

In Ireland, all General Practitioners (GPs) operate privately and either the state or the individual pays for access to this care. The State pays in full for access to the GP for around 39%[113] of the population, either through the Medical Card or GP Visit Card.[114] Where an individual does not qualify for a Medical Card under the income guidelines,[115] they can apply for provision to be made on a discretionary basis.[116] Under official guidelines, the HSE may give regard to "additional guideline allowances", which include non-income related criteria such as medical condition.[117] However there are concerns about transparency in determining Medical Card eligibility on a discretionary basis.[118] Significant geographic inconsistencies in how they have been allocated are apparent; for example an individual living in North Cork is almost six times more likely to receive a discretionary Medical Card than one in Dun Laoghaire.[119] Despite the provision for income-based and discretionary Medical Cards, a report by the Combat Poverty Agency indicates that almost 22% of people living in consistent poverty and 30% of people at risk of poverty did not have a Medical Card in 2006.[120] The study indicated that some of the factors in those people not having Medical Cards included the role of discretion in the awarding of cards, income thresholds that were too low,[121] lack of targeting of cards to those in greatest need and lack of information about entitlement including language and literacy issues.[122] In 2009, nearly 50,000 people living in consistent poverty and 199,000 people at risk of poverty did not have a Medical Card.[123] Clearly the existing provision for Medical Cards is not meeting the needs of all those living in poverty or at risk of poverty. There are significant numbers of individuals falling through the gaps.

DEFINITIONS OF CONSISTENT POVERTY AND AT RISK OF POVERTY

Official definitions of poverty are as follows[124]:

The official Government-approved poverty measure used in Ireland is consistent poverty, developed independently by the Economic and Social Research Institute (ESRI). This measure identifies the proportion of people, from those with an income below a certain threshold (less than 60% of median income), who are deprived of two or more goods or services considered essential for a basic standard of living. The 'at risk of poverty' indicator identifies all those (households or people) who fall below a certain income threshold, which in the EU has been set at 60% of the median income.

For those not entitled to free care – 61% of the population – payment is made by them to the GP directly, through out-of-pocket payments, on a pay per visit basis.[125] GP consultation fees can vary significantly around the country from €35 – €70.[126] The Resource Allocation Group found that for non Medical Card holders, having no direct subsidy for GP services is "unique compared with other developed countries" and places particular burdens on people who are just above the Medical Card/GP Visit card thresholds and/or who require regular contact with their GP.[127] There have been a number of studies that have shown that people avoid going to their GP because of the cost.[128] The cost of access to GP care acts as a "serious disincentive to people to attend primary care, particularly for lower income groups."[129] In a recent survey by Millward Browne 19% of people polled stated that they or a family member have been denied or delayed access to healthcare because of inability to pay for a healthcare service.[130]

Significantly, social class is a key factor in whether you have ever been denied or delayed access to healthcare services.[131] Of those denied or delayed access to care, the figures were as follows: Class AB, 9%; C1, 16%; C2, 21%; D, 25%; E, 24%, and; F, 9%.[132] Class AB are most likely to be covered by private insurance, and Class F by Medical Card provision. It is those between the two that can face greatest difficulty.

- Access to Acute Care

The arrangement in place for accessing acute care (see box on categories of patient entitlements above) ensures that no-one treated under the public health system is expected to pay the full cost of their treatment. Any costs incurred are billed to the patient and though in theory it is treated the same as any other household bill[133] there is in fact legislation in place to ensure that hospitals can waive the bill in cases of undue hardship.[134] There are, however, indications that the current arrangement of healthcare in Ireland results in cost being a barrier to accessing acute care. Assessing how cost acts as a barrier to people accessing care at acute level is difficult as there is very little data kept on access to healthcare in private hospitals.[135] However, the following provides a snapshot to demonstrate instances where cost is a barrier to accessing acute healthcare.

An individual's ability to access timely and affordable healthcare can depend on whether they have private health insurance. In 2007, Medical Card holders were three times as likely to be on in-patient waiting lists and twice as likely to be on outpatient waiting lists as privately insured patients.[136] The Expert Group found that "individuals who can afford private health insurance gain access to some hospital services faster than those with equivalent health needs but who do not have insurance."[137]

55% of individuals with private health insurance coverage belong to the ABC1 group whereas only 10% of those with private health insurance belong to the lowest socio-economic group. Though, traditionally, health insurance has been relatively affordable in Ireland, this is changing. Since 2004, the average cost of private health insurance has risen by 45.3%, with an increase of 11.5% in 2008 – 2009 alone.[138] Added to this, the country is experiencing an economic crisis and rising unemployment. One impact of this is a significant number of people can no longer afford health insurance. The number of people with private health insurance decreased by approximately 42,000 between June 2009 and June 2010.[139] A reduction in private insurance coverage may increase the numbers seeking to access public healthcare services.

- Waiting for healthcare

Waiting lists for access to healthcare are a persistent feature of the Irish healthcare system, and one that exemplifies the inequality within that system.[140] *Quality and Fairness* promised to increase the capacity of the health system in Ireland in an effort to reduce waiting lists. One of the most controversial issues has been separate waiting lists for public and private patients. This is commonly referred to as a two-tier system – where there are different levels of access to healthcare for private patients and public patients. The national health strategy acknowledges that the mix between public and private practice is a contributory factor in the unacceptably long waiting lists for public patients.[141] A recent study suggests that the over-utilisation of public hospital beds by private patients may indicate that the treatment of private patients is being favoured over the medical need of public patients. The use of public hospital beds by privately insured patients is problematic where any over-utilisation results in delays in care for public patients.[142]

SKIPPING THE QUEUE

Patients with entitlement only to access public healthcare services can face longer waiting times. But they can speed up their access to public healthcare services if they can afford to pay for one-off private healthcare services, such as diagnostic testing. Patients with private health insurance can access both private healthcare services, and public healthcare services. The services they access may in fact be delivered in the public system, thereby reducing the capacity available to patients with only public healthcare entitlements.

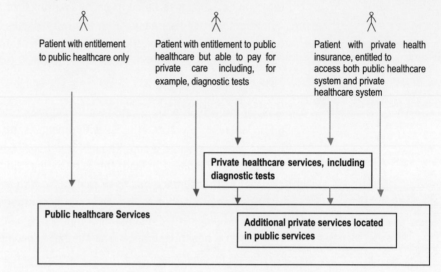

Ireland was urged by the Committee on Economic, Social and Cultural Rights, in 2002, to introduce a common waiting list for public and private patients in public hospitals.[143] The previous government implemented a number of strategies to reduce hospital waiting times and committed to such a common waiting list for private and public patients in public hospitals.[144] However, the impact of these initiatives on access to healthcare is not always clear and waiting lists remain a problem in Irish hospitals.[145] One initiative in place since 2002 is the National Treatment Purchase Fund, (NTPF). This is a dedicated fund, used for the sole purpose of purchasing treatment in private hospitals for public patients who have waited more than three months from their out-patient appointment.[146] Individuals contact the NTPF to see if they are eligible for this scheme. The NTPF then sources treatment for qualifying patients in hospitals in Ireland. Patients who opt for treatment with the NTPF receive their treatment free of charge.[147] In 2009, the average wait time for patients prior to receiving treatment on the NTPF was approximately seven months.[148] Since its introduction it has been successful in addressing waiting lists for certain procedures.[149] The overall impact, however, has been limited. In 2008, for example, only 3.17% of public patients were treated using the National Treatment Purchase Fund.[150]

In the Programme for Government, Government for National Recovery 2011-2016[151], it was announced that a Special Delivery Unit would be established in the Department of Health to assist the Minister in reducing waiting lists. Discussions are ongoing as to the future role of the National Treatment Purchase Fund, but the Minister for Health confirmed that the Fund has been asked to "cease further commitments to patients until the special delivery unit was in place and decided how best resources to cut waiting lists should be used."[152]

A significant problem is that data on the differential waiting times for Medical Card and privately insured patients is not collected annually, making it very difficult to track trends. This is part of a general lack of data on waiting times. Recently, the Health Information and Quality Authority (HIQA) proposed the introduction of standardised templates to address inadequate data gathering in the GP referral process.[153] Until this is implemented, an accurate picture of waiting times will be incomplete.[154] The lack of disaggregated data on waiting times also prevents any analysis of how economic factors are linked to access to healthcare and health outcomes in Ireland.

- Using resources to deliver economic access to care

No matter whether a healthcare system is private or public, or a mix of the two, the government is responsible for ensuring that access to healthcare is affordable and timely and available without discrimination. Maximum available resources are to be used to progressively realise the right to health, including equal access. It must be noted that maximum available resources is more than the totality of allocations in the annual budget process – it includes all government resources, including resources foregone through tax expenditures (tax breaks) in the budget. Tax expenditure is one of the ways in which government support for different policy goals may not be visible in its direct budget expenditure.

In Ireland, a number of tax expenditures relate to the healthcare system including tax relief for individuals purchasing private health insurance premiums or in relation to specific individual medical expenses. Tax relief is also granted by the state for the construction of private hospitals. Initially tax breaks were introduced in the Finance Act of 2001 for hospitals run by charitable organisations. These tax concessions were then extended to private hospitals in 2002.[155] From 2002, capital allowances were available for the construction or refurbishment of buildings used as or to be used as private hospitals.[156] Provisions in the Finance Act 2009[157] terminated this scheme, although provision was made for transitional arrangements. Statements from the Minister for Finance have indicated the cost to the state in terms of income tax foregone: "For each €100 million of qualifying capital expenditure on these hospitals, the cost of tax relief to investors (assuming a marginal tax rate of 41% for those investors) would amount in gross terms to €41 million spread over 7 years or approximately €5.9 million per annum over that 7 year period."[158] In 2008 alone, 339 claims were made in relation to €30.1 million capital allowances for the construction of private hospitals; this accounted for €12.3million in income tax foregone.[159] In 2005 the then government also introduced tax break concessions for private hospitals co-located on the grounds of public hospitals. As part of the conditions for tax relief these hospitals were required to make 20% of their beds available to public patients. The government stated that this was intended to be on a cost neutral basis to the state though no cost benefit analysis was undertaken. This is consistent with the general approach to tax expenditures in Ireland.[160] To date there is no evidence that additional capacity in public health services has been available to public patients. What is not clear is whether these tax expenditures by the State, albeit in the form of tax expenditure rather than direct spending, was the most appropriate way to increase capacity in acute healthcare that would be available to the population on an equal basis regardless of ability to afford private healthcare insurance.

In examining the use of resources on healthcare, it is clear that the provision of tax reliefs focused on the health sector is part of the State's contribution to funding health, even if not included in the health spend per se. The tax expenditures outlined above illustrate how government has allocated resources towards private healthcare. This care is only available to individuals who can afford private health insurance. This has occurred against a backdrop of insufficient provision for others to access affordable care, including insufficient provision for Medical Card and GP Visit Cards for those living in poverty and ongoing waiting lists for people dependent on public healthcare.

The Expert Group on Resource Allocation was critical of the use of tax expenditures to underpin healthcare financing: "Tax reliefs lack transparency and are generally inefficient in terms of targeting government resources. The resources currently spent on tax reliefs could be devoted more usefully to direct and targeted subsidies for access to community based care and reduced costs for drugs to enhance equity and integrated care. Since private health insurance is mainly focused on episodic hospital care the tax reliefs provided do little to encourage integrated care models and they reduce equity. The resources involved could be employed more usefully to improve policy related objectives."[161]

SECTION 4: ENFORCING THE RIGHT TO HEALTH IN IRELAND

The right to health, like any right, requires that states are accountable. This means having effective, transparent and accessible monitoring and accountability mechanisms. Ireland has ratified six of the nine core UN human rights conventions, including the International Covenant on Civil and Political Rights (ICCPR) and the ICESCR, both in 1989. Having ratified these conventions, Ireland, as a 'State Party', is bound under international law to observe their provisions. However, international law does not become enforceable in Ireland unless and until it is incorporated into Irish law.

4.1 THE ROLE OF COURTS AND OTHER BODIES

There is no express recognition of health as a human right in the Irish Constitution or legislation. In the case of *Heeney v Dublin Corporation*,[162] the Court recognised "there is a hierarchy of constitutional rights and at the top of the list is the right to life, followed by the right to health".[163] However, in *In the Matter of Article 26 of the Constitution and the Health (Amendment)(No. 2) Bill 2004*,[164] it was argued that a constitutional right to healthcare could be derived from the right to life, the right to personal dignity and/or the right to bodily integrity. The Court rejected the existence of a right to health where that would create an obligation upon the state to provide free healthcare.[165] While the right to health in international law similarly does not create a right to free healthcare, this judgement reflects the overall resistance by the Supreme Court to the recognition of economic, social and cultural rights, and their enforcement.[166]

Accountability does not have to rely solely on judicial remedies – there can also be administrative channels of accountability. Relevant quasi-judicial and administrative bodies can be charged with overseeing the delivery of the State's human rights obligations. The Irish Human Rights Commission's mandate covers the full spectrum of Ireland's human rights obligations and it can undertake individual cases and enquiries, in addition to its advisory function to government.

While the Irish Human Rights Commission has an express mandate as the national human rights institution, other administrative bodies like Ombudsman and complaints bodies can also carry out an oversight or adjudicative role on human rights.

States can also sign up to UN and regional individual complaint mechanisms. The Optional Protocol to the International Covenant on Economic, Social and Cultural Rights, when in force, will provide individuals with a right of petition to the CESCR. This Optional Protocol has not been signed or ratified by Ireland at the time of writing.

4.2 INDIVIDUAL REMEDIES FOR HEALTHCARE IN IRELAND

In 2007, a new statutory complaints system for the HSE came into effect[167]. Anyone receiving public health or personal social services in Ireland may make a complaint about the actions or failures of the HSE, their service providers, or HSE contractors who provide services on behalf of the HSE. *Your Service Your Say* provides a Complaints Service for issues concerning care, treatment and practice.[168] The HSE also has an Appeals Service to provide an "independent review of decisions taken by personnel of the HSE relating to applications by members of the public for specified services and entitlements, where applicants are dissatisfied with the outcome of their application."[169] This appeal process includes decisions on eligibility for Medical Cards. There are concerns about the value of this appeals process, considering the mechanism for further appeal, the Office of the Ombudsman, is not an adjudicatory body and it can only recommend rather than enforce remedial action.

The Office of the Ombudsman in Ireland is mandated to investigate complaints about the administrative actions of government departments, and the HSE.[170] Individuals can complain about delays in providing services, the refusal to award a benefit or service. The Ombudsman is empowered to look at whether the actions being complained about are, for example, taken without proper authority, on irrelevant grounds, or are discriminatory. They can then ask the body about whom the complaint has been made to review what it has done, change its decision and/ or offer the individual an explanation, an apology, and/or financial compensation.[171]

The Ombudsman has expressed concern that the HSE accounted for more than a quarter of the complaints from the public dealt with by the Ombudsman's office in 2009.[172] The Ombudsman has also stated that she has had significant problems in trying to elicit information from the HSE, recently describing events that the HSE initiated as "frustrating, wasteful, dispiriting and, ultimately, useless" and further claiming that they "undertook what appeared to be a deliberate attempt to prevent publication of [an] investigation report."[173] It is also important to note that the outcome of any investigation by the Ombudsman is in the form of recommendations, which are not binding on the body to which they are directed.

There is evidence to suggest that current mechanisms are not effective means of accountability. According to a public poll in 2010 only a third of those who experienced healthcare provision below expectations made a complaint; 84% reported some degree of difficulty in knowing who to complain to and 52% felt intimidated in some way about making a complaint.[174]

SECTION 5: CONCLUSIONS AND RECOMMENDATIONS

Ireland has been a party to the International Covenant on Economic, Social and Cultural Rights for over 20 years. Yet, as this briefing paper has outlined, Irish law and policy does not make sufficient provision for the right to health. While there is extensive health policy expertise in Ireland, both at the level of those formulating it and those offering critique, what is missing is the incorporation of the human rights framework as it applies to health. A critical first step in delivering on the right to health in Ireland is understanding what the right means and what is required of Government.

Irish law and policy, including the national health strategy, must be based on the right to health. The human rights framework does not dictate the particulars of Government healthcare policy, but it does require equity of access. This is not being delivered for people living in Ireland. Government must ensure that cost is not a barrier to care and that socio-economic status does not determine the timing of care. Evidence indicates that the current provision for free healthcare is insufficient, with people falling outside the current parameters facing financial barriers in accessing care. Similarly, individuals not availing of private health insurance face delays in accessing care.

Realisation of the right to health also requires that the Government has in place effective monitoring and accountability mechanisms and that individuals whose right to health is violated have access to effective remedies. In Ireland the lack of a Constitutional or legislative provision on the right to health removes the possibility of any judicial remedy given the lack of appetite to develop common law jurisprudence on the right to health from other existing provisions like the right to life. The existing oversight mechanisms for the healthcare system are not sufficiently robust. Greater accountability mechanisms for healthcare would allow for testing of the State's asserted commitment to fair access.[175] The implementation of recommendations around data collection and collation are critical insofar as any monitoring of the operation and performance of the health service and the impact on individuals requires that the appropriate information is available.

Delivering on the right to health in Ireland will require more than addressing the single question of economic access, or simply increasing the overall spend on healthcare. Rather, it is time for Ireland to map the way in which it delivers healthcare, including how it ensures that people are able to access care that is affordable and without undue delay, against the human rights obligations that it has signed up to.

➢   **Using the right to health as the basis for delivering healthcare in Ireland**

1.   Review healthcare and the health system on the basis of human rights standards, and develop action plans to implement treaty provisions;

2.   Frame national health policy and the national health strategy around the right to health, specifically the four components for health facilities, goods and services – availability, accessibility, acceptibility of good quality. Following the conclusion of *Quality and Fairness* in 2011, the next national health strategy must be based on these requirements, and include clearly defined indicators and benchmarks to measure progress to deliver upon the right to health. The data should be disaggregated on the basis of age, gender, income, ethnicity and rural/urban dwelling at a minimum;

3. Ensure all Government departments consider health outcomes in relation to policy and practice, to deliver an integrated health system in recognition of the social determinants of health;

4. Ensure public participation in all health-related decision making at community, national and international levels;

➢ **Ensuring that cost is not a barrier to care**

5. Ensure that all individuals have equal access to timely and quality healthcare services and that no one is denied or delayed access to healthcare services by policies or practices that have the purpose or effect of discriminating on the basis of ability to pay;

6. Ensure that fees for health services, whether publicly or privately set, do not prevent individuals from obtaining the healthcare that they need without undue delay;

7. Allocate resources to healthcare consistent with human rights obligations, including transparency around maximum available resources;

8. The Government must address the findings and recommendations of the Expert Group on Resource Allocation, including a time-bound review of that report, and transparency as to those recommendations which will be implemented, those which will not, and rationale for those decisions. Such a review must be based on the economic access requirements under the state's obligations on the right to the highest attainable standard of physical and mental health;

9. Provision of and eligibility for Medical and GP Visit Cards must be reviewed against Ireland's human rights obligations, to ensure that there is sufficient provision for individuals for whom cost is a barrier to care;

➢ **Greater accountability for delivering the right to health**

10. The Government must incorporate the provisions of the ICESCR, including a right to access healthcare, into Irish law, either through Constitutional or legislative provision;

11. The Government should include information on access to healthcare services, specifically economic access, in their reports to UN treaty bodies and in its report under Universal Periodic Review, and should implement subsequent recommendations;

12. Ireland must sign and ratify the Optional Protocol to the ICESCR, recognising the competence of the Committee on Economic, Social and Cultural Rights to receive complaints from individuals in Ireland;

13. National accountability mechanisms must be brought into line with human rights standards;

➢ **Data collection and collation to ensure health services are designed to deliver the right to health**

14. The Department of Health and Children and the Health Service Executive must track, assess and publicly report on trends in economic access to care. Disaggregated data collection and analysis should be improved to better identify and develop responses to cost as a barrier to care, and differences in access to care without undue delay between individuals accessing healthcare services, for example waiting times for accessing services based on public or private provision.

REFERENCES

1   Committee on Economic, Social and Cultural Rights, General Comment 14, The right to the highest attainable standard of health, 2000, UN Doc. E/C.12/2000/4

2   International Covenant on Economic, Social and Cultural Rights (ICESCR), 1966, UN Doc. A/6316 (1966) Article 12

3   Mervyn Susser, 'Health as Human Right: An Epidemiologist's Perspective on Public Health' (1993) 83, 3 American Journal of Public Health, p.418

4   General Comment 14 on the right to health represents an authoritative statement of what the right to health encompasses. See General Comment 14 of the Committee on Economic, Social and Cultural Rights (CESCR), E/C.12/2000/4, 11 August 2000. Available at: http://www.unhchr.ch/tbs/doc.nsf/(symbol)/E.C.12.2000.4.En. (Hereinafter CESCR, General Comment 14)

5   CESCR, General Comment 14, para. 8

6   CESCR, General Comment 14, para. 17

7   CESCR, General Comment 14, para. 36

8   ICESCR, Article 2(1)

9   CESCR, General Comment 14, para. 12

10 Amnesty International, Human rights for human dignity. A primer on economic, social and cultural rights, London, 2005, p.3

11 ibid. at 41

12 Hunt, P (2008) Report of the UN Special Rapporteur on the Right to Health (A/HRC/7/11)

13 CESCR, General Comment 14, para 19

14 Commission on Human Rights, Economic, Social And Cultural Rights, Report of the Special Rapporteur on the right of everyone to the enjoyment of the highest attainable standard of physical and mental health, Paul Hunt, 2005, UN Doc. E/CN.4/2005/51, at 58

15 Fundar-Centro de Análisis e Investigación, International Budget Project and International Human Rights Internship Program, Dignity Counts, a guide to using budgetary analysis to advance human rights, 2004, p.2

16 Ibid

17 Committee on Economic, Social and Cultural Rights, General Comment 3, The nature of states parties obligations (Art. 2, par. 1), 1990, UN Doc. E/1991/23

18 CESCR, General Comment 14, para 37

19 "A state has a legal obligation to ensure that a health system is accessible to all without discrimination …[this means] that outreach (and other) programs must be in place to ensure that disadvantaged individuals and communities enjoy, in practice, the same access as those who are more advantaged." Paul Hunt & Gunilla Backman (2008). 'Health Systems and the Right to the Highest Attainable Standard of Health.' Health and Human Rights, 10(1) : 81-92, p83

20 CESCR, General Comment 14 para 57 – 58. See also Paul Hunt (2003). 'The Right of Everyone to the Highest Attainable Standard of Physical and Mental Health. UN Doc A/58/427, 10 October 2003

21 ICESCR, Article 2(1)

22 Office of the High Commission for Human Rights, Factsheet 31: Right to health, p.24

23 CESCR, General Comment 14, para 43

24 Marta Santos Pais (former Chair of the UN Committee on the Rights of the Child and Director of the UNICEF Innocenti Research Centre), A Human Rights Conceptual Framework for UNICEF, UNICEF Innocenti Essays No. 9, 1999, p. 8.

25 For a more comprehensive explanation of the principle of non-discrimination in international human rights law see Amnesty International, Dealing with Difference: A Framework to Combat Discrimination in Europe, 2009 (Index: EUR 01/003/2009)

26 Article 15 of the ICESCR provides the right of the individual to enjoy the benefits of scientific progress and its applications

27 CESCR, General Comment 14, at 18

28 Committee on Economic, Social and Cultural Rights, General Comment No. 20, Non-Discrimination in Economic, Social and Cultural Rights (art. 2, para. 2), 1999, UN Doc. E/C.12/GC/20, at 35

29 CESCR, General Comment No. 20

30 Human Rights Committee, General Comment No. 18: Nondiscrimination, 1989, para. 13

31 CESCR, General Comment 14 at 43(f) and 54

32 Office of the United Nations High Commissioner for Human Rights, Principles And Guidelines For A Human Rights Approach To Poverty Reduction Strategies, Geneva, 2006, para. 76 and 77

33 World Health Organisation (2010). World Health Statistics Report 2010. Geneva, Switzerland: WHO Press, p48 - 54

34 World Health Organisation (2010). World Health Statistics Report 2010. Geneva, Switzerland: WHO Press p50

35 Deaths from circulatory diseases are 16.5% lower than the EU average, whereas cancer mortality is 5.5% higher than the EU average. Department of Health & Children (2010). Health in Ireland: Key Trends 2010. Dublin, Ireland: Department of Health and Children, p17-18

36 Our Geels, All Ireland Traveller Health study, Dublin, Department of Health and Children, 2010, Summary Findings, p.80. This study, published in 2010, is the most recent comprehensive information on Traveller health

37 Life expectancy at birth for male Travellers has remained at the 1987 level of 61.7 which is 15.1 years less than men in the general population, representing a widening of the gap by 5.2 years. Life expectancy at birth for female Travellers is now 70.1 which is 11.5 years less than women in the general population, and is equivalent to the life expectancy of the general population in the early 1960s. See Our Geels, All Ireland Traveller Health study, Dublin, Department of Health and Children, 2010, Summary Findings, p.85

38 Life expectancy at birth for male Travellers has remained at the 1987 level of 61.7 which is 15.1 years less than men in the general population, representing a widening of the gap by 5.2 years. Life expectancy at birth for female Travellers is now 70.1 which is 11.5 years less than women in the general population, and is equivalent to the life expectancy of the general population in the early 1960s. Traveller infant mortality is estimated at 14.1 per 1,000 live births. This is a small decrease from an estimated rate of 18.1 per 1,000 live births in 1987. Over the same time period the general population infant mortality rate has reduced from 7.4 to 3.9 per 1,000 live births. This is based on a Traveller population in the island of Ireland estimated at 40,129 in 2008; 36,224 in the Republic of Ireland and 3,905 in Northern Ireland. See Our Geels, All Ireland Traveller Health study, Dublin, Department of Health and Children, 2010, Summary Findings, p.87

39 This is both a global and Irish trend. For example, the Commission on Social Determinants of Health found that "In countries at all levels of income, health and illness follow a social gradient: the lower the socioeconomic position, the worse the health." Closing the gap in a generation: health equity through action on the social determinants of health. Final Report of the Commission on Social Determinants of Health. (2008). Geneva, World Health Organization, Executive Summary. For an Irish analysis, see Richard Layte & Brian Nolan (2004). 'Equity in the Utilisation of Healthcare in Ireland.' The Economic and Social Review, Vol. 35, No. 2, Summer/Autumn, 2004, pp. 111–134

40 Layte, R, Nolan, A and Nolan, B (2007) Poor Prescriptions: Poverty and Access to Community Health Services: CPA, Dublin, at xxi

41 Ibid

42 Central Statistics Office (2010). Survey on Income and Living Conditions 2009. Dublin, Ireland: CSO, p42

43 Department of Health and Children, *Quality and Fairness: A Health System for You, Health Strategy*, 2001, Dublin, Ireland: Government Publications

44 Committee on Economic, Social and Cultural Rights (2002). *Concluding Observations of the Committee on Economic, Social and Cultural Rights, Ireland*. Un Doc E/C.12/1/Add.7, 5 June 2002, para 35. "The Committee recommends that the State party review the recently published National Health Strategy with a view to embracing a human rights framework in that strategy, in line with the principles of non-discrimination and equal access to health facilities and services, as outlined in paragraph 54 of General Comment No. 14"

45 The statutory agency responsible for the execution of health policy, administration and management of services

46 Expert Group on Resource Allocation and Financing in the Health Sector (2010). *Report of the Expert Group on Resource Allocation and Financing in the Health Sector*. Dublin, Ireland: Government Publications

47 Expert Group on Resource Allocation and Financing in the Health Sector (2010). *Report of the Expert Group on Resource Allocation and Financing in the Health Sector*. Dublin, Ireland: Government Publications, at 107

48 OECD Health Data 2010 - Frequently Requested Data, Paris, 2010, Total expenditure on health data
    Organisation for Economic Cooperation and Development, Health at a Glance: Europe 2009, Paris, 2009, p163

49 Organisation for Economic Cooperation and Development, Health at a Glance: Europe 2010, Paris, 2010, Chapter 4: Health Expenditure and Financing

50 Written answer by Mary Harney (Minister, Department of Health and Children; Dublin Mid West, Independent) to Parliamentary Question by Caoimhghín Ó Caoláin (Cavan-Monaghan, Sinn Fein) 8 July 2010

51 8.7% versus an OECD average of 9.0%. Even when USA, the country responsible for the largest percentage expenditure, is removed from the OECD comparison, Ireland is still below the average. Organisation for Economic Cooperation and Development (2010). *Health Indicators at a Glance 2009*. p163

52 Maev Ann Wren (2003). *Unhealthy State: Anatomy of a Sick Society*. Dublin, Ireland: New Island. p236, p376. For example, spending on community welfare services are accounted for in health spending under Vote 40 of the Revised Estimates for Public Services, Department of Finance, 2010

53 In 2008, €18.839bn of total expenditure was made up of €15.172bn in total public health gross expenditure, €1.262bn in private insurance spending, €2.289bn of out-of-pocket expenditure, and €116 million on private investment. (Written answer by Mary Harney (Minister, Department of Health and Children; Dublin Mid West, Independent) to Parliamentary Question by Caoimhghín Ó Caoláin (Cavan-Monaghan, Sinn Fein) 8 July 2010) While full disaggregated data is not available for 2009, the full spend was €19.7bn in total, with €15.44bn in public health expenditure. (Aoife Brick, Anne Nolan, Jacqueline O'Reilly and Samantha Smith (2010). *Resource Allocation, Financing and Sustainability in Healthcare: Evidence for the Expert Group on Resource Allocation and Financing in the Health Sector, Volume 1*, p.17.)

54 Written answer by Mary Harney (Minister, Department of Health and Children; Dublin Mid West, Independent) to Parliamentary Question by Caoimhghín Ó Caoláin (Cavan-Monaghan, Sinn Fein) 8 July 2010

55 Irish Nurses and Midwives Organisation, Privatisation of the Irish Health Care System, INMO Position Paper 2010, Dublin, 2010, p.11

56 "There is no framework which allows decisions to be taken in an integrated way that links systematically with the overarching principles of the Irish health care system and aligns resources with goals" Expert Group on Resource Allocation and Financing in the Health Sector (2010). *Report of the Expert Group on Resource Allocation and Financing in the Health Sector*. Dublin, Ireland: Government Publications, page x

57 Ibid. at xi (emphasis added). "In relation to the financing of the health-care system, the Group found that the current financing system lacks transparency, gives rise to serious inequities in access to care, and results in numerous anomalies in terms of incentives for users of care."

58 Hunt, P (2008) Report of the UN Special Rapporteur on the Right to Health (A/HRC/7/11), p.12, Citing A. Green, An Introduction to Health Planning for Developing Health Systems, Oxford University Press, 2007, p.64

59 For example, in 2006, the Health Service Executive warned Tallaght hospital about its designation of private beds, having found that over 40 percent of the beds in the public hospital were being used to treat private patients. See Burke, supra note 10, at 118

60 Department of Health and Children, *Quality and Fairness: A Health System for You, Health Strategy*, 2001, Dublin, Ireland: Government Publications, pg. 100, "Under the present arrangements, 80 per cent of beds in acute hospitals may be currently designated as public while 20 per cent may be private."

61 Health Service Executive, Consultant Contract (2008), section 2(d) and 2(e)

62 Department of Health and Children, *Quality and Fairness: A Health System for You, Health Strategy*, 2001, Dublin, Ireland: Government Publications

63 The 2004 Act states that, in performing its functions the HSE shall have regard to '… policies and objectives of the Government or any Minister of the Government.'63 Monthly performance reports are submitted to the Minister for Health and Children, as part of the reporting requirements of the Act.63 Under the 2004 Act each year the government allocates resources to the HSE under Vote 40. The HSE is required to submit an annual service plan to the Minister for approval and that plan must be in accordance with the policies and objectives of the Minister and of Government. The plan is subsequently submitted to both houses of the Oireachtas. The HSE must provide its services as set out in the Annual Service Plan within the agreed budget

64 Indecon, Review of Government Spending on Mental Health and Assessment of Progress on Implementation of a Vision for Change. Submitted to Amnesty International Ireland, 2009, p84

65 Department of An Taoiseach, Government for National Recovery 2011-2016, Dublin, 2011, pg. 32, available at http://www.taoiseach.gov.ie/eng/Publications/Publications_2011/Programme_for_Government_2011.pdf

66 This information is adapted from the clear outline of healthcare services in Expert Group on Resource Allocation and Financing in the Health Sector (2010). *Report of the Expert Group on Resource Allocation and Financing in the Health Sector*. Dublin, Ireland: Government Publications, pg. 46/47

67 Under the Maternity and Infant Care Scheme, every women who is pregnant and ordinarily resident in Ireland is entitled to maternity care. Women are entitled to this service even if not eligible for a Medical Card. This includes a certain level of ante-natal and post-natal GP visits, free in-patient and out-patient **public** hospital services in respect of the pregnancy and the birth, without liability for any of the standard in-patient hospital charges, and provision for infant care services. See http://www.hse.ie/eng/services/Find_a_Service/maternity/combinedcare.html

68 Department of Health & Children (2001). Quality & Fairness: A Health System for You. Dublin, Ireland: Stationary Office

69 Speech by Mr. Micheál Martin TD. Launch of Health Strategy, 26 November 2001. Available from www.dohc.ie/press/speeches/2001/20011126.html

70 Expert Group on Resource Allocation and Financing in the Health Sector (2010). *Report of the Expert Group on Resource Allocation and Financing in the Health Sector*. Dublin, Ireland: Government Publications, p. 50 "there is a shortage of certain types of public acute hospital capacity in Ireland, resulting in unsustainably high occupancy rates." Occupancy rates in some acute hospitals are over 90 per cent where the recommended norm (based on international experience) would be no more that 85 per cent. This has been linked, by the same group, as linked to existing patterns of service delivery within Irish healthcare

71 For example through co-location and the National Treatment Purchase Fund

72 See General Comment 14 at 18-19 for full details of enumerated rights

73 CESCR, General Comment 14 at 18

74 CESCR, General Comment 14 at 43

75 CESCR, General Comment 14, 43 (e)

76 CESCR, General Comment 14 at 43(f) and 54

77 Primary Care: A New Direction (2001)

78 Department of Health & Children (2002). *Promoting Women's Health – A Population Investment for Ireland's Future*

79 Department of Health & Children (2002). *Traveller Health: A National Strategy 2002 – 2005*

80 *Strategic Taskforce on Alcohol 2002; Report of the Working Group on Treatment of Under 18 olds Presenting to Treatment Services with Serious Drug Problems* (2005)

81 *National Strategy for Action on Suicide Prevention* (2005); *Tackling Chronic Disease - A Policy Framework for the Management of Chronic Diseases* (2008), *A Vision for Change: Report of the Expert Group on Mental Health* (2006)

82 More older people live in rural areas than in urban locations. 52% of people living in rural areas report difficulty in accessing public transport compared to 11% in urban areas. Central Statistics Office, 2007, and 2009

83 Value for Money and Policy Review of Efficiency and Effectiveness of Long-Stay Residential Care for Adults within the Mental Health Services (2008) shows that 81.9% of the provision of community care services is in urban areas p.12, that there were 845 inpatient and community-based beds in Dublin Mid Leinster 793 in Dublin North East, 1,513 in the South 1,501 in the West and 57 in Central Mental Hospital

84 All Ireland Traveller Health Study Team at the School of Public Health, Physiotherapy and Population Science, University College Dublin (2010). *All Ireland Traveller Health Study: Our Geels*. Dublin, Ireland: Department of Health and Children, p76

85 Report of the Task Force on the Travelling Community, 1995

86 See, for example, Immigrant Council of Ireland (2010). *Submission to the Special Rapporteur on the Human Rights of Migrants on access to economic and social rights by migrants – particularly the enjoyment of the right to adequate standard of living (Article 11 of ICESCR) and right to health (Art. 12 ICESCR) for undocumented immigrants in Ireland*

87 These include length and continuity of residence in Ireland or other parts of the Common Travel Area, length and purpose of any absence from Ireland or the Common Travel Area, nature and pattern of employment, their main centre of interest, their future intentions to live in Ireland as it appears from the evidence. See Citizens Information Bureau (2010). Available from htttp://www.citizensinformation.ie/en/social_welfare/irish_social_welfare_system/social_assistance_payments/residency_requirements_for_social_assistance_in_ireland.html>

88 Migrant Rights Centre of Ireland, Submission to Annual Thematic Report of Special Rapporteur on Human Rigths of Migrants to the Human Rights Council, January 2010, available at www.mrci.ie

89 Cairde (2006). Assessing the Health & Related Needs of Minority Ethnic Groups in Dublin's North Inner City. A Case Study of a Community Development Approach to Health Needs Assessment. Available from http://www.cairde.ie/wp-content/uploads/2009/08/Assessing_the_Health_and_Related_Needs_of_Minoirty_Ethnic_Groups.pdf 54% of respondents believed they were entitled to a Medical Card, 32% believed that they were not entitled, 14% of respondents did not know the status of their entitlement (p40), 18% of respondents who were unsatisfied with their health attributed their dissatisfaction to financial constraints or lack of a Medical Card (p42)

90 The at risk of poverty rate is 12.3% when the head of the household is male, compared to 17.1% for a female head of household. The average net disposable household income of female-headed households was €39,413 compared to €50,750 for households headed by males. Central Statistics Office (2010). *Survey on Income and Living Conditions (SILC) 2009*. Dublin, Ireland: Stationary Office, p41, p16

91 Report on the Consultation for the National Action Plan against Poverty and Social Exclusion 2006 – 2008 (2006). Dublin, Office of Social Inclusion, p10

92 CESCR, General Comment 14, at 12 (b) (iii)

93 Ibid

94 Ibid, at 34

95 Ibid, at 35

96 Ibid, at 36

97 Ibid, at 52

98 Determination of eligibility for a Medical Card is the responsibility of the Health Service Executive (HSE) and there are three primary means of determining eligibility: means test, discretionary assessment and EU Entitlement. Both the means test and the discretionary assessment are based on the concept of avoiding 'undue hardship', to an individual if they had to pay their own medical costs. EU entitlement is the result of agreements with EU countries on access to healthcare

99 Health Service Executive, Medical Card / GP Visit Card National Assessment Guidelines, 2009

100 The current, as at March 2011, standard daily charge for in-patient care is 75 euros, up to an annual maximum of 750 euros. Emergency department visits are free, if referred by a GP, otherwise charged at a rate of 100 euros. See Hospital charges, http://www.hse.ie/eng/services/Find_a_Service/Older_People_Services/Benefits_and_Entitlements/Hospital_charges.html In 2009, emergency admissions accounted for 62% of inpatient treatments, Health Service Executive, *Annual Report & Financial Statements 2009*, 2010

101 Health Service Executive, Monthly Performance Report 2011, March 2011, Medical Cards: 1,648,818; GP Visit Cards: 120,050

102 The Health (Amendment) No. 2 Bill 2010, introduced the legislative basis for charges to be made in respect of prescription items dispensed to medical card holders. A charge of 50 cent is imposed in respect of prescription items dispensed by a community pharmacy contractor on foot of a prescription issued under the GMS (Medical Card) Scheme. Certain categories of person will be exempt from the charges, and there are limits on the level of charges that can be incurred in a month

103 Expert Group on Resource Allocation and Financing in the Health Sector (2010). *Report of the Expert Group on Resource Allocation and Financing in the Health Sector*. Dublin, Ireland: Government Publications, pg 44. Medical Card holders were exempt from paying the Health Levy and from the Income Levy introduced in 2009. However, they are not exempt from the Universal Social Charge introduced in 2010, to replace these two levies

104 Expert Group on Resource Allocation and Financing in the Health Sector (2010). *Report of the Expert Group on Resource Allocation and Financing in the Health Sector*. Dublin, Ireland: Government Publications, pg 44

105 The over-70s became eligible as a blanket group under 2001 Health (Miscellaneous Provisions) Act, with a separate, higher, income threshold. In 2009 the automatic entitlement for the over-70s was removed and means testing applied under the *Medical Card national Assessment Guidelines for Persons aged 70 Years and Older*

106 Expert Group on Resource Allocation and Financing in the Health Sector (2010). *Report of the Expert Group on Resource Allocation and Financing in the Health Sector*. Dublin, Ireland: Government Publications, pg 44

107 Ibid

108 Ibid. The proportion of people who do not have a Medical Card or private health insurance includes those individuals who only have a GP Visit Card.

[109] GP surgery ranges from €35 to €70 at time of publication, with no regulation of permissible fee levels. National Consumer Agency, 2010, Doctors and Dentists Survey

[110] Any costs incurred are billed to the patient. Previous government policy was that this was to be treated as typical household bill, "They will be billed by the hospital administrator and will pay the bill in due course, as they pay other bill in their family or as part of other responsibilities" Oral response from Brian Cowen (Taoiseach, Laois-Offaly, Fianna Fáil) to Parliamentary Question from Eamonn Gilmore (Dún Laoighaire, Labour), 4th November 2008. However, there is legislation in place to ensure that hospitals can waive the bill in cases of undue hardship (Section 4(b)4 Health (Amendment) Act 2005 "The HSE may reduce or waive a charge imposed on a person if it is of the opinion that, having regard to the financial circumstances of that person, it is necessary to do so in order to avoid undue financial hardship in relation to that person"). There is no indication of what process the HSE has for determining this and how often it is used as a basis for waiving hospital fees. In 2009, €324,637,454 was collected in total hospital fees with €175,382,282 outstanding (Parliamentary Affairs division to PQ 31431/10 by James Reilly TD, 8 July 2010)

[111] CESCR, General Comment 14, para 9 "*primary healthcare* typically deals with common and relatively minor illnesses and is provided by health professionals and/or generally trained doctors working within the community at relatively low cost; *secondary healthcare* is provided in centres, usually hospitals, and typically deals with relatively common minor or serious illnesses that cannot be managed at community level, using specialty-trained health professionals and doctors, special equipment and sometimes in-patient care at comparatively higher cost; *tertiary healthcare* is provided in relatively few centres, typically deals with small numbers of minor or serious illnesses requiring specialty-trained health professionals and doctors and special equipment, and is often relatively expensive."

[112] Note, as it is beyond the scope of this briefing to look at all aspects of primary care, the focus will be on GP care

[113] Health Service Executive, Monthly Performance Report 2011, March 2011, Medical Cards: 1,648,818; GP Visit Cards: 120,050

[114] Individuals who do not qualify for a Medical Card on income grounds may also qualify for a GP Visit Card. This was introduced in 2005, and is means tested at a 50% higher income level. If an individual applying for a GP visit card is above the income guidelines, the HSE must consider if refusing eligibility would result in it being 'unduly burdensome' for the individual to access healthcare for themselves or their family (Health Act 1970 section 58). See Health Service Executive (2009). 'Medical Card / G.P. Visit Card National Assessment Guidelines,' Available from < http://www.hse.ie/eng/services/Find_a_Service/entitlements/Medical_Cards/mcgpvcguidelines.pdf > p37. GPs may become a contractor with the PCRS under the HSE to facilitate the free entitlements of GMS card holders. Participating GPs are remunerated under the terms of the Health Professional (Reduction of Payments to General Practitioners) Regulations 2009. See www.pcrs.ie

[115] Health Service Executive (2009). 'Medical Card / G.P. Visit Card National Assessment Guidelines,' Available from <www.hse.ie/eng/services/.../Medical_Cards/mcgpvcguidelines.pdf> p9, p60 Income guidelines have not been revised since 2005

[116] Discretionary cards amount to 5% of total Medical Cards (80,524 as of December 2010). However, this proportional figure is likely to be an underestimate of the actual number of discretionary cards in the system due to the fact that a certain amount of discretion is involved when assessing any individual's eligibility under the HSE Medical Card Guidelines. (Discretionary GP Visit Cards (17,501 as of December 2010) amounted to 15% of total visit cards issued to date. Health Service Executive (2011). Monthly Performance Report December 2010. Available from <http://www.hse.ie/eng/services/Publications/corporate/HSE_Monthly_Performance_Reports_.html> p23

[117] HSE (2009). Medical Card / GP Visit Card National Assessment Guidelines, p38

[118] Fundamentally, ability to pay can affect access to health in Ireland. The rationale behind decisions to provide free access to some and not others is not always clear. The Expert Group found "widespread anomalies" in the current Long Term Illness system which provides free access to healthcare for individuals with conditions on the Long Term Illness list. (Expert Group on Resource Allocation and Financing in the Health Sector (2010). *Report of the Expert Group on Resource Allocation and Financing in the Health Sector.* Dublin, Ireland: Government Publications, at xi) While some important diseases are covered, equally serious ones are not, with no clear rationale for the difference in provision

[119] http://www.medicalindependent.ie/page.aspx?title=major_inconsistencies_in_discretionary_medical_cards

[120] Patricia Keilthy (2006). *Medical Card Eligibility: Profiling People Living in Poverty without a Medical Card using EU-SILC 2006*, Combat Poverty Agency Working Paper Series 09/04, p3

[121] i.e. where the income threshold is lower than the rates for measuring poverty and therefore people living in poverty but just above the income threshold do not qualify or assume they will not be eligible and therefore don't apply

[122] Ibid

[123] Central Statistics Office (2010). *Survey in Income and Living Conditions (SILC).* Dublin, Ireland: Stationary Office. The CSO uses a combination of income and material deprivation indicators to determine levels of poverty, in line with the NAPS definition. There is no comparable research on the 2009 data like the Keilthy 2006 study above to outline the reasons for these continuing figures of unmet need for Medical Cards by those living in or at risk of poverty

[124] http://www.socialinclusion.ie/poverty.html

[125] These payments can be reclaimed against income taxation at a standard rate of 20 per cent

[126] National Consumer Agency (2010). *Doctors and Dentists Surveys, May 2010.* Available from <http://www.nca.ie/eng/Research_Zone/price-surveys/NCA-Doctors-Dentists-Report-may2010.doc> p11-12

[127] A recent study identified that over 50% of adults without Medical Cards have deliberately not visited their doctor when feeling ill due to financial considerations. See Expert Group on Resource Allocation and Financing in the Health Sector (2010). *Report of the Expert Group on Resource Allocation and Financing in the Health Sector.* Dublin, Ireland: Government Publications p66 and p70

[128] Nolan, A (2006) 'Evaluating the Impact of Eligibility for Free Care on the Use of GP Services in Ireland: A Difference-in-Difference Matching Approach', ESRI, ISSC & University of Ulster Working Papers No.25; Nolan A and B Nolan (2007) 'The Utilisation of GP Services' in Nolan B et al (eds) The Provision and Use of Health Services, Health Inequalities and Health and Social Gain, ESRI. Available from <http://www.esri.ie/publications/search_for_a_publication/search_results/view/index.xml?id=2259>
Dermot O'Reilly, Tom O'Dowd, Karen J. Galway, Andrew W. Murphy, Ciaran O'Neill, Ethna Shryane, Keith Steele, Gerry Bury, Andrew Gilliland, Alan Kelly (2007). 'Consultation Charges In Ireland Deter A Large Proportion Of Patients From Seeing The Gp: Results Of A Cross-Sectional Survey.' *European Journal Of General Practice*, 13: 231-236

[129] Expert Group on Resource Allocation and Financing in the Health Sector (2010). *Report of the Expert Group on Resource Allocation and Financing in the Health Sector.* Dublin, Ireland: Government Publications, at 66

[130] Amnesty International, Attitudes to Healthcare and Public Spending, Omnibus Survey, Fieldwork: 1st – 11th September 2010, © Millward Brown Lansdowne: September 2010

[131] Ibid. Of those denied or delayed access to care, the figures were as follows: Class AB, 9%; C1, 16%; C2, 21%; D, 25%; E, 24%, and; F, 9%. Signficantly Class AB are most likely to be covered by private insurance, and Class F by Medical Card provision. It is those between the two that can face greatest difficulty

[132] These categories are used by the polling organisation, Millward Brown Lansdowne, based on the profession of the chief income earner in the household of the individual polled. As such, Class AB would be professions including accountant, barrister, senior civil servant, individual living off investments or private income, surveyor or newspaper editor / journalist. Class C1 would include bank clerks, nurses, teachers; C2 is skilled working class and includes entry-level policy officer, chef, plumber; D is other working class such as postman, docker or housekeeper. F is those on lowest level of subsistence including lowest grade workers, those in retirement whose only income is state support, and those unable to work dependent on state supports. Class F is broken down into large- and small-holding farmers

[133] 4th November 2008 Dail Debate Brian Cowen in response to Eamonn Gilmore question on inpatient fees "They will be billed by the hospital administrator and will pay the bill in due course, as they pay other bill in their family or as part of other responsibilities"

[134] Section 4(b)4 Health (Amendment) Act 2005 "The HSE may reduce or waive a charge imposed on a person if it is of the opinion that, having regard to the financial circumstances of that person, it is necessary to do so in order to avoid undue financial hardship in relation to that person"

In 2009, emergency admissions accounted for 62% of inpatient treatments (HSE (2009). *Annual Report & Financial*

[135] Expert Group on Resource Allocation and Financing in the Health Sector (2010). *Report of the Expert Group on Resource Allocation and Financing in the Health Sector.* Dublin, Ireland: Government Publications, at 203

[136] CSO (2008). *Quarterly National Household Survey: Health Status and Health Service Utilisation*, p16

[137] Expert Group on Resource Allocation and Financing in the Health Sector (2010). *Report of the Expert Group on Resource Allocation and Financing in the Health Sector.* Dublin, Ireland: Government Publications, at 66 p xi

[138] Parliamentary Question No 26168/10, Bernard Durkan to Mary Harney, 17 June 2010

[139] The Health Insurance Authority (2010). *Newsletter: August 2010 edition.* Available from <http://www.hia.ie/latest-news/newsletters.htm>

[140] HSE Performance Report, December 2010

[141] Department of Health and Children, *Quality and Fairness: A Health System for You, Health Strategy*, 2001, Dublin, Ireland: Government Publications, pg. 100

[142] O'Reilly, J. and Wiley, M. (2010). 'Who's that sleeping in my bed? Potential and actual utilization of public and private in-patient beds in Irish acute public hospitals.' *Journal of Health Services Research and Policy*, 15(4) pp 210-214

[143] Committee on Economic, Social and Cultural Rights, Concluding Observations of the Committee on Economic, Social and Cultural Rights : Ireland, 2002, UN Doc. E/C.12/1/Add.77, para. 35 " Committee furthermore urges the State party to introduce a common waiting list for treatment in publicly funded hospitals for privately and publicly insured patients."

[144] According to the HSE "status on the common waiting list will be determined by clinical need only",HSE, 2009, *Public and private patients in public hospitals: Guidance to health service management on the treatment of public and private patients*

[145] O'Regan, Eilish (2010). 'HSE Orders an End to 'Two-Tier' Waiting Lists.' Irish Independent [online]. February 16, 2010. Available from http://www. independent.ie/health/latest-news/hse-orders-an-end-to-twotier-waiting-lists-2064773.html "Public hospitals have been banned from asking patients booking diagnostic tests if they have private health insurance...In internal correspondence, Health Service Executive (HSE) chief executive Brendan Drumm instructed one of his senior executives to inform hospitals about the new rule..."Common waiting lists should be in place. There was also the issue of our HSE-paid staff being involved in asking questions in relation to private practice, which should be an issue of serious concern to us," he said."

[146] Quality and Fairness, p101

[147] www.ntpf.ie

[148] Comptroller and Auditor General, Accounts of the Public Services 2008, Dublin, 2009, p.485

[149] A total of 164,449 patients were treated under the NTPF between 2002 and 2009 and the median waiting time on the NTPF list for medical and surgical patients is now 2.5 months. See National Treatment Purchase Fund, Annual Report 2009, Treating Patients Faster, Dublin, 2010, pp. 9 and 18

[150] Comptroller and Auditor General, Accounts of the Public Services 2008, Dublin, 2009, pg. 350

[151] Department of An Taoiseach, Government for National Recovery 2011-2016, Dublin, 2011, pg. 32, available at http://www.taoiseach.gov.ie/eng/Publications/Publications_2011/Programme_for_Government_2011.pdf

[152] Reilly unveils new agency to tackle hospital waiting lists, Irish Times, 1 June 2011

[153] Health Information & Quality Authority (2010). *Standardising Patient Referral Information: A Draft National Template for Consultation.* Available from <http://www.hiqa.ie/media/pdfs/HI_patient_referral.pdf> Accessed 16 December 2010

[154] Patient waiting times are not acknowledged in official statistics until that patient has been waiting for more than 3 months. "It has long been the practice, under several Governments, not to include patients waiting for hospital treatment for less than 3 months in published waiting list statistics." Written Answer from Mary Harney to James Reilly, 17 October 2007

[155] Section 31 Finance Bill 2002

[156] (Finance Act 2001, section 64, in effect May 2002.)

[157] Finance Act 2009 section 8

[158] (Written answer by Brian Lenihan Jnr (Minister, Department of Finance; Dublin West, Fianna Fail) to Parliamentary Question by Caoimhghín Ó Caoláin (Cavan-Monaghan, Sinn Fein), 28 October 2008.)

[159] (Written answer by Brian Lenihan Jnr (Minister, Department of Finance; Dublin West, Fianna Fail) to Parliamentary Question by Tommy Broughan (Dublin North East, Independent), 13 October 2010)

[160] "While there are criteria for capital expenditure in the Department of Finance, with spending of over €30 million requiring full cost-benefit analysis and with other criteria applying too, major public expenditure through the granting of tax incentives to investors was not subject to such evidence-based analysis until very recently." Paul Sweeney, Deconstructing and Annual Budgetary Process, Dublin, 2011, para. 24. This is not only the case in forecasting of costs but generally in monitoring costs. "In the case of many, if not most, tax expenditures the Revenue Commissioners are not required to collect information on the use and cost of these expenditures while the Department of Finance, in its annual reports, monitor only a handful of high profile, and high cost, tax expenditures." Micheál Collins and Mary Walsh, Ireland's Tax Expenditure System: International Comparisons and a Reform Agenda, The Policy Institute, Dublin, 2010, , p. 2. The Commisison on Taxation recommended "better measurement and data collection of the costs and benefits associated with the introduction or extension of the tax expenditure and the review of its impact. This is an essential prerequisite to tighter measurement and control of public resources." Commission on Taxation, Part 8: Review of Tax Expenditures, Dublin, 2009, p.230

[161] Expert Group on Resource Allocation and Financing in the Health Sector (2010). *Report of the Expert Group on Resource Allocation and Financing in the Health Sector.* Dublin, Ireland: Government Publications, pg. 119-120

[162] Heeney v. Dublin Corporation [1998] IESC 26 (17th August, 1998), at para. 16. The case was taken by a group of tenants in the Ballymun social housing high-rise flats complex, who claimed the local authority at the time was obliged, under their tenancy agreement, to provide a reasonably efficient lift service. The court accepted that this was the case

[163] Irish Human Rights Commission, (2005) Making Economic, Social and Cultural Rights Effective: An IHRC Discussion Document, Dublin, IHRC, p.110

[164] Unreported Supreme Court decision of 16th February 2005

[165] Irish Human Rights Commission, (2005) Making Economic, Social and Cultural Rights Effective: An IHRC Discussion Document, Dublin, IHRC, p.110

[166] Ibid

[167] As set out in Part 9 of the Health Act (2004)